THE (IN)FIDELITY FACTOR

Points to Ponder *Before* You Cheat

Elda M. Lopez

EML & Co.
Los Angeles, California

THE (IN)FIDELITY FACTOR: Points to Ponder *Before* You Cheat

Published by EML & Co.
Los Angeles, California
www.emlandco.com

Contact info: www.eldamlopez.com

ISBN-13: 978-0-578-12159-8

Printed in the United States of America

Relationships/Self Help/Personal Growth

Dedicated to:

My parents, Frances and Alfred Lopez, married 41 years.

Though they reside in infinity –

my love knows no bounds…

Table of Contents

Preface

When I first had the idea to write this book I received some interesting feedback. One friend asked, "Are you okay?" He obviously assumed that I must be out of my mind to tackle such a complex subject matter as fidelity. Another inquired, "What's gotten into you?" Probably for the same reason as friend number one. Honestly, I just got tired of reading yet another sensational headline about the latest scandal of fidelity gone awry.

Political figures, captains of industry, devout Christians, A-Z list actors, your Uncle Joe, the local grocer and everyone else in between are susceptible to slipping away from fidelity while in a committed relationship. This issue encompasses every color, creed, class, and intellect. Maserati or turnip truck—*in*fidelity proves to be a great equalizer. It's quite evident that emotional intelligence and common sense are not mutually inclusive where an impressive I.Q. and worldly accomplishments are concerned. We've all heard, know, or have been personally affected by the fall-out from indiscretions. Not pretty.

For the record, I am not an expert. I am a practicing human and have a B.A. in Theatre Arts, not degrees in psychology. Although psychology was an area of study that I frequented, I am by no means a true learned student. However, the theater of the absurd that is being played out loud these days, namely, the unfailing lack of fidelity and accountability in committed relationships, got me seriously thinking. I have concerns regarding this condition running amuck in our society, and most importantly—the lack of *personal* accountability. People cheat, move on, leave a tattered trail behind them and repeat the cycle ad nauseam. It seems cheating has almost reached pop culture status, except pop culture can be entertaining, cheating—not so much.

I've had my fair share of experiences with fidelity and infidelity. Not proud of some situations, ahead of the game on others. I will not likely compromise my values again. I'm choosing to use my frontal lobe for good. Like the rest of us I've made mistakes large and small. I'll undoubtedly continue to blunder in other areas, personal evolution being what it is—ongoing.

With lessons learned come awareness and responsibility. Whether you are the recipient of fidelity gone wrong or the one coloring outside the lines, you are culpable on some level. Innocent parties are rare in these situations. I realize that's a hard pill to swallow, but it's true. I know, I had that pill stuck in my throat a time or two.

I understand there are not altogether simple solutions for conditions that may prove to be more complicated and outside the scope of everyday thought. We all have a history. Some are more dark than others. Some histories contribute to chronic hesitancy and internal apprehension that prevent one from inner exploration and outward forward motion, which in turn leads to unhealthy patterns; infidelity being one of them. This book does not fully address the multipart, steadfastly rooted backstories that inhibit and sometime cripple personal growth. If you find yourself in this category, seek trained advisors to address these issues, or read books that may prove beneficial as stepping stones toward living a more complete life. Do *something*; start with baby steps to help release your limitations. Fortunately, a segment of this particular population has overcome deep-seated injuries that stem from a troubled upbringing, abuse, or other debilitating events. These folks have reclaimed themselves through intense self-reflection, self love, faith, mental health counseling, support groups, etc. And you can, too.

The main objective of this book is to present enough useful information, statistics, surveys, and factual life narratives in order to stimulate intelligent thought, or at the very least, *practical* thought in regards to fidelity, commitment, and accountability.

Honor yourself: read on, to stay strong.

Acknowledgments

Fortunately my experience with this project has been relatively smooth due to the helping hands along the way. An abundance of appreciation goes out to family and friends who offered their invaluable feedback, encouragement, and support. I'm indebted to those who shared their very personal stories. It took bravery, and I'm sure a fair amount of discomfort, even under the cloak of anonymity. My appreciation goes out to the participants in my survey. The information shared gives a voice to everyday people. A very special heartfelt thanks goes out to D.J.D., for many reasons.

I am much obliged to Tawanda Majoni, Cathy W. Meyer, Victor Villasenor and Dr. Herb Goldberg. Their respective articles and quotes added to the enterprise at large. I'd like to highlight the various websites that allowed their content usage. I gleaned a lot of necessary info from these pages. They are too numerous to name, but I have referenced them in the book.

This work was pulled together by many talented and qualified people. I have listed them in the resource guide. Their knowledge and skill filled in my numerous blanks. Creating the written word can be quite a challenge. If you're inclined to give it a go, please give them considerable thought.

I'd like to recognize those who are helping to avert infidelity via example, education, spiritual guidance, or simple wise words. This topic deserves reinvigorated attention. Hopefully some will pick up the book and move resolutely forward in their lives.

Introduction

This book is for those with a desire to know and those in the throes of desire.

Specifically if:

- You are in a committed relationship or are contemplating one; a relationship where there is to be no hanky-panky outside the perimeters unless one party or the other discusses otherwise, and it is *mutually* agreed upon that other steps may be taken to reframe, resolve, or dissolve the relationship.

This book may not be for you if:

- You have an actual medical condition, addiction, etc., that requires a specific regime or antidote.
- You have an open relationship.
- You have a non-committed relationship.
- You have an "understanding" and guidelines for your relationship that do not include fidelity and commitment in the traditional sense.

This book is not about snobservations, judging, bias, or religious bents, although certain examples have been made in order to stress salient points. The main purpose of this book is to serve as a reference for those whereby fidelity is the mainstay of their relationship. The content deals mainly with male/female relations since I have no experience in any other area to speak to, or from. However, whatever your bonding preferences are, please track accordingly and take away what you can. Ideally this is everybody's guide to a better understanding of fidelity and its components, and there are quite few. It's a little more intricate than just saying I will/I do and jumping in. The intent is to examine fidelity in a user-friendly way. There is plenty of material out there written by psychologists with varying scholarly degrees and licenses that provide tremendous help and keen insight, while also introducing skills and tools to deal with troubling life issues.

With regards to this particular book, the hope is that by providing other essentials and food for thought, merely leafing through these pages will provide positive gains. We all deserve that, at the very least. So, please follow along in your hymnals…

Disclaimer

This book is designed to provide information about the subject matter covered. It is sold with the understanding that the publisher and author are not engaged in rendering legal, accounting, or other professional services. If expert assistance is required, the services of a competent professional should be sought. It is not the purpose of this book to reprint all the information that is otherwise available to authors and other creative people but to complement, amplify, and supplement other texts.

Every effort has been made to make this book as complete and as accurate as possible. However, there may be mistakes both typographical and in content. Therefore, this text should be used only as a general guide and not as any sort of ultimate source. The purpose of this manual is to educate and entertain. The author has neither liability nor responsibility to any person or entity with respect to any loss or damage caused or alleged to be caused directly or indirectly by the information contained in this book.

Please read responsibly.

fidelity: fi-del-i-ty [fi-**del**-i-tee]

1. strict observance of promises, duties, etc.
2. loyalty.
3. conjugal faithfulness.
4. adherence to fact or detail.

Many persons have a wrong idea of what constitutes true happiness. It is not attained through self-gratification but through fidelity to a worthy purpose.

—Helen Keller

Faithful women are all alike, they think only of their fidelity, never of their husbands.
—Jean Giraudoux

Most men find it difficult to be true to one woman, but relatively easy to be true to three or four at the same time.
—Georges Courteline

Do not let loyalty and faithfulness forsake you; bind them around your neck, write them on the tablet of your heart.
—Proverbs 3:3

Chapter 1

The Basics

Fidelity within a committed relationship can be quite the challenge. Romantic relationships are one of the most confounding and profound experiences you can have; tricky business to be sure. However, any kind of quality relationship requires fidelity: work, family, friend, romance. Relationships also entail good amounts of give and take—plenty of shifting between those two. The goal is balance. Balance to some is an unknown concept, but it's certainly a model worth discovering and fighting for, which in turn contributes to the overall lasting effects of fidelity and commitment. The strived for win-win.

It can be said there are three main types of romantic alliances. Not science, mere observation.

1) The exception to the rule(s). This very, *very* rare breed is supernaturally preordained from the get-go. They were deemed by the magic wand to couple and stay coupled. It just works. Period.

2) Those who form a bond whereby one is willing to take a back seat to the other to some extent. Their version of balance

is relative yet workable. They seem happy and content with their roles.

3) Everyone else: those who care enough to work toward their best, those who question, are uncertain, confused, clueless, who renounce or are blinded by the roles and supposed rules of conventional relationships. A fair amount of work goes into these relationships—hopefully.

Now onto the learning curve…

Once upon a time in a land far, far away there lived the quaint notions of fidelity and commitment. These notions lived in lofty minds and tender hearts. The commitment of which I speak entailed mates who entered into a union unto each other, a supposedly forever thing. Official vows, legality, and the eyes of God were usually involved. This particular concept of commitment (agreement, pledge, dedication) included the emotional and physical kind. Such as: I commit to be your mate solely. I commit to loving and lusting only for you. I commit to honoring our agreement within the bounds of our relationship. Then a funny thing happened along the way to fidelity, although the humor is somewhat lacking…mates stopped being responsible to their word, and all-hell-pretty-much-broke-loose. Que pasó? Well, let's take a look.

Fidelity. Hopefully you took a hard look at the definition(s) provided. Please do stay alert, there'll be a test later, namely the one you apply to yourself. Let's examine this word, fidelity, as it applies to married couples: conjugal faithfulness. Now let's examine it as it applies to otherwise committed individuals: loyalty. There's also the definition of strict observance of promises and duties. The word strict may seem harsh, but for the sake of argument we'll use it. At the very least it implies structure. Of course, however a couple chooses to define strict and structure within the comfort of their nest is entirely up to them. We've been told that religion and the law hold rights in that department, but it's become painfully obvious that humans will do what humans will do.

The meaning of fidelity seems pretty clear, right? Not a lot of room for a loose interpretation. Not *kinda* like being a faithful wife/husband. As in, but honey, the company insisted I wine and dine (heavy on the wine) this client five nights a week. And, not kinda like being a loyal mate. As in, sweetie, it was just a kiss—that lasted till the wee hours of the morning in the back seat of...our car. And certainly not like, "I swear it was an accident!" Oh, so you accidentally fell *into* her/*onto* him while you were both naked. Yeah, not like that.

Fidelity in a committed relationship is well defined in order to secure the boundaries. Countries secure their boundaries to ward off interlopers and war. Relationships share some of the same principles, though the boundaries are not meant to be oppressive, repressive, or possessive. Fidelity serves to bond mates and families, not to impose bondage and servitude. There can be a huge disconnect in relation to the purpose and the practice. The limits are set by willing parties to protect and preserve the integrity of the relationship. By the way, should you find yourself in an oppressive relationship, be mindful in recognizing that this is not by any means healthy or acceptable. Do your best to find an alternative solution—it exists, don't ever doubt that! Communication, compassion, and patience are some of the best tools for relationship-building, and bonus: they've actually been known to work once you *commit* to them.

I imagine a good number of people pride themselves in possessing fidelity beyond reproach. We profess our undying love at the altar (hotel, gazebo, grassy meadow, shore, cave) and expect the same in return from our mate. We proudly, sometimes smugly, think our borders are secure. We're not those people who would do otherwise. We follow rules, we pay taxes. We love God and country. We put forward due diligence as human beings. We teach and preach high standards, morals, and principles to our children and to anyone else who will listen. The sacred vows have been said, 'til death do us part, and are meant. Well…yes, and sometimes not in the most honorable of ways. Murder and mayhem have reared their ugly heads a time or two…or three, in regards to the unfaithful, but for now let's just stick to good old-fashioned death by natural causes. As we know, forever is a very, very long time to be committed. A fair amount of folks don't entirely comprehend what that means. So, is it any surprise that all our moral high falutin'-ness is brought to its proverbial knees via a little thing called reality? Nope. Unless of course you live in some super universe where there is no fury in a woman scorned and emotionally evolved men are the norm. Truth is, we fall short in relationships, and do so miserably at times. Herein, welcome infidelity.

Infidelity has made quite a name for itself. I trust you read this definition as well. Remember, there'll be a test—unfortunately, a substantial portion of the populace will likely fail this one, or excel, depending on how you look at it. Infidelity is having its glory days with all the high-profile people of late that have fallen prey to its siren call. And that's only the froth of the latte. What about all the regular Joes and Janes that engage in this behavior? I'm guessing big numbers across the board. Infidelity seems to be gaining momentum. Nobody thus far has been able to rein it in effectively. No vow, no legal paper, no religious doctrine, no government, no amount of money; no person, place, or thing. Pigs may actually fly in hell as it freezes over before it's under control.

Okay, so now we have: commitment, fidelity, and its unruly twin, infidelity. These are the big headliners. Not many get off the planet without a dose of these in various forms. You're either in compliance, struggling with, or coming to terms with one or the other. Wherever you find yourself, each carry their own unique set of circumstances and struggles. Side bar: if you're one of the scant few who truly have a blessed union without much ado, well, happy, happy, joy, joy for you! I mean that! You are extraordinary indeed. Keep up the good work and do hold your fellow brothers and sisters in your thoughts and prayers. We can all use as many well-wishes as we can get. Nevertheless, it wouldn't hurt to continue reading. Having some information is better than not…just in case.

It seems fairly conclusive that humans possess a weak link within the commitment department. How about we do a comparative survey of our friends in the animal world? Let's take a peek at the who's who of monogamy in the kingdom. The following sampling was largely provided by Mother Nature Network (www.mnn.com) and of course, who would know better?

<u>The A-List</u>

Gibbons: nearest relatives to humans that mate for life

Swans: monogamous bonds for years, sometimes for life

Black vultures: known to attack a philanderer

French angelfish: always in pairs, as a team defend territory against other pairs

Wolves: family life more loyal and pious than human relationships

Albatross: will return to the same place and partner

Some species of termites: King and Queen bear the entire kingdom

Prairie vole: cited as animal model for human monogamy

Turtle doves: emblems of love and faithfulness

Bald eagles: nobility in monogamy

Schistosoma mansoni worms: parasites that form life bonds *inside* the human body

Granted, some of these animals will take on another mate if theirs is infertile or dies, but their fidelity scores are higher by far than us mere Homo sapiens. I don't know about you, but I'm a bit embarrassed that a parasitic worm that invades the human body and reproduces therein is more trustworthy than the head honcho it's feeding off of. Think about it. An unpleasant creature enters into our biological system, finds its soul mate, bears equally offensive offspring (sorry, Mother Nature), and lives happily ever after. How many romantic evenings are we playing host to? How many toasts of champagne? How many family outings? Meanwhile, said host is off being a knucklehead and getting into all kinds of trouble for having less prudence than its uninvited guest. How's that for food for thought?

On the other hand, we have the bonobos. These active primates do not form permanent monogamous sexual relationships. They are a very friendly great ape found in the Democratic Republic of the Congo. Very friendly. They're known for their high levels of sexual behavior. They interact with each other freely and don't seem to discriminate with regards to sex or age. The beauty being there is no jealousy, competition, aggression, etc. Unlike humans. They have sex for conflict appeasement, affection, social status, excitement, and stress reduction. Not unlike humans. Bonobos are also thought to be matriarchal. Females tend to collectively dominate males by forming alliances and use sexuality to control them (no comment). A male's rank in the social hierarchy is often determined by his mother's rank. These guys are known for having the attributes of compassion, altruism, empathy, kindness, patience, and sensitivity. They're also known to be relatively peaceful as a whole. Not a bad group of apes. One could actually admire them. I rather like the fact they're matriarchal. Imagine a world where women know best, but that's a whole other book.

Another tribe, the Mosuo, who happen to be human, have their own exclusive set of relational customs. They hail from the Yunnan and Sichuan Provinces in China. I first heard of them while watching an episode of *Taboo* (the following excerpted material, not necessarily in order, is brought to you by Wikipedia. Please refer to the site for more details and annotated notes. It's quite a read.). All ongoing sexual relationships in Mosuo culture are called "walking marriages." These bonds are based on mutual affection. When a Mosuo woman or man expresses interest in a potential partner, it is the woman who may give the man permission to visit her. These visits are usually kept secret, with the man visiting the woman's house after dark, spending the night, and returning to his own home in the morning. Mosuo women and men can engage in sexual relations with as many partners they wish. There is no established marriage in this culture. Therefore there are no husbands, wives, or permanent mates.

While a pairing may be long-term, the man never lives with the woman's family, or vice versa. Mosuo men and women continue to live with and be responsible to their respective families. The couple do not share property. The father usually has little responsibility for his offspring. "It is the job of men to care more for their nieces and nephews than for their own children." A father may indicate an interest in the upbringing of his children by bringing gifts to the mother's family. This gives him status within the mother's family, while not actually becoming part of the family. Whether or not the father is involved, children are raised in the mother's home and assume her family name. They are considered to be matrilineal (hmmm…a running theme).

So, we've gone from one end of the spectrum to the other. Where do, we, humans extraordinaire, lie in the grand scheme of things?

Well, there is the argument that humans are not meant to be monogamous. We are primal beings after all. We have base instincts and work off them. We would undoubtedly do more of that if it weren't for laws, religion, and your mom. Humans are blessed with a highly developed brain and are capable of abstract reasoning, language, introspection, problem solving, not to mention self-awareness and rationality. Hard to claim innocence (ignorance is another matter) when we've reached this level of intelligence.

I can understand the humans-aren't-meant-to-be-monogamous argument. It makes sense on some levels. However, we are discussing fidelity. This is a man-made word that was created with intent and has been defined. It only stands to reason that if you're going through all the pomp and circumstance of committing, i.e., professing love on bended knee, throwing lavish ceremonies, signing polished pre-nups, breaking glasses, jumping brooms, or any and all versions of the above—then do so. Commit. You gave your word, your love, your heart, your soul. To what degree can be argued later, but at that moment, you gave your all. And it's that moment that defines who you've agreed to be relative to your partner.

Technically you have chosen to unite with another via all the mighty and magnificent words that have sprung from judges, Elvis impersonators, Unitarian Universalist ministers, your personal sonnets, and assorted devout passages of your preferred religion. You really, really mean it. You are the pride and joy of all who witness this sacred event. Little Jimmy is all grown up; a man now. Little Susie: a lovelier blushing bride there has never been. True love. All around there are tears of joy and smiles of deep pleasure and satisfaction. Honey, we've sent our child off into the happily-ever-after. We've done good, can't wait for the begetting to start. The lineage will grow strong and robust, our gift to society.

Cut to: mmmm…a few months to five years down the line. Houston, we have a problem. The love launch has gone wrong. Little Jimmy fancies himself as Big Jimbo, and Little Susie, please call me Susannah, have made their way onto the path of least resistance. It seems the vows that fell so breathlessly and lovingly from their lips have become uncomfortably lodged within their throat. In fact, there's almost no memory recall whatsoever. Tabula rasa. Certainly no memories come to mind whilst in the arms of some new paramour recounting the Kama Sutra for the fifth time. Problem? What problem? I'm fine. I've got a bit on the side to help me through my stresses. It's just a temporary thing. So-and-so will never find out, besides he/she doesn't really care or understand what I'm going through, anyway.

Enter the seven warps: stress, guilt, anxiety, remorse, projection, reaction, and utter dissatisfaction—the new bedfellows. Make room, paramour. Now what? Lies, deceit, and secrecy—even better. What could have been avoided by addressing the issues beforehand has now taken on a very negative twist. Shame, fear, anger, revenge, bitterness, resentment, the list goes on and on and on…are taking their toll. Shattered dreams, families, and egos are the by-product. Communication is virtually non-existent. The divorce lawyer is your new BF. There goes the house, cars, kids, bank accounts, civility. Let the nightmare begin.

Predictably, it's all very heartrending and grievous. The issues that could have been brought to light stayed within the shadows far too long. Unfortunately most were missed in the first round. Infidelity is typically the final round, but it doesn't have to be. Believe it or not there is an upside. There is hope for mending and healing through therapy/counseling, support groups, homework, patience, and understanding, while trying to piece back the trust. We'll expound more on this later. Sadly, the common scenario is that the infidelity cycle continues in some form because it takes full-frontal courage to do otherwise. Not bravado, courage. Who's got the cojones?

Chapter 2

I Do

Prince Charming and Cinderella meet, greet, and marry. Mr. and Mrs. Charming had the perfect life and marriage. They loved, honored, and obeyed like nobody's business. In sickness they were divine, nary a snivel or a whine. In health, forget about it. They were the happiest, shiniest people ever. In their presence birds twittered, brooks babbled, and flowers competed for the best bloom.

Prince Charming was exactly that, plus, he never groused, overworked or released offensive odors. He was sound of body and mind. No issues, no extra body tissue. He was coiffed and clothing coordinated. He adored his wife unconditionally and with his vast knowledge of lovemaking, he was equal parts sensual and sinful.

Little Miss Cindy definitely held her own. She, of the movie star looks, was also intelligent, vibrant, attentive, even-tempered, nurturing, an epicure extraordinaire, a breadwinner in her own right, and glorious in their private chambers.

Life was dreamy. All was right in their world, until...The End—The Bitter End. The prince is off with Rapunzel and Cinderella is left with Rumplestiltskin, or vice versa. It was only a fairytale?! But, it was such a great story! Mirror mirror on the wall, relationships aren't fantasies after all.

Prince-maybe-not-so-charming and Lady C have become another statistic. The odds makers are howling and counting their lucre. It's payday, baby! yet again. Alas, it was just a matter of time. All that I Do hype and false pretense has seen another day. Matrimonial hyperbole: a cycle perpetuated that proves equally damaging. Another precursor to fidelity falling by the wayside.

I DO, three letters that can impact one's life in both positive and negative ways. We're taught from the get-go that when one says, I Do, that's it, you *do*. You do promise to honor, cherish, _____ (fill-in-the-blanks). Nothing wrong with that, unless of course they're merely words without merit, which according to some statistics is about 49 percent of the time. Marriage is commitment with a bold, italicized capital ***C***: that grand old institution of everlasting love, heavenly propagation, immaculate picket fences—and a pile of groceries, laundry, bills, and debt. Conventionally, marriage has been the cornerstone of all that is strived for. Find your ideal partner, build a life, make a few babies, and you're on your way to gifts and glory. Easy peasy. Religion exalts, the law mandates, and society and family influence. Where's the problem? Refer to the previous...we are still promoting the pristine fantasy of marriage.

Marriage in its purest form is a thing of beauty. Truly. The intent here is not to take away from this celebrated ritual. However, its untidiness is neatly and conspiratorially tucked away. Someone forgot to factor in the human condition. The holy sacrament of matrimony has shed its former splendor and has come forth as an undeniable force to be reckoned with. Its merits can't be stressed enough, yet the lack of candor has been stretched too far. With all due respect, marriage in the loosest sense is a bit like communism; in theory it looks pretty darn good, in application—well, you be the judge.

Religion for all its well-referenced goodness still places an extremely high price on the holiness of marriage. That's all fine and dandy, except no one is getting down and gritty with it. You have to back it up with authentic facts, as well as with the word of _____ (your favored deity here). If religion is going to set the tone for marriage, where is the "reality" responsibility? Isn't there a moral responsibility to discuss marriage in accurate, genuine terms as well? Logically and thoughtfully speaking, it seems they should not be mutually exclusive.

Traditional society, still a stronghold, dictates: get married, do the right thing. For some, it's the only thing. Family says: hurry so we don't have to worry. Find a mate, settle down, lead a normal life, and please stay married. The law steadfastly sets the standards and the escape clauses. The outward message in each instance appears to be, statistics be damned; carry on and ignore the fact that marriage is a full-time job that no one is sufficiently trained for, which then opens the door for unconstructive behavior. Stating the obvious, we *all* need to step up our game.

Unfortunately, there aren't many who teach about the everyday realities of what fidelity means and what a true committed relationship is about. Marriage and relationships in and of themselves supply no real tools. We are not taught how to be with another individual day in and day out. There are no manuals for this. No course of action that gives helpful hints on how to handle someone who is cranky, messy, and rude. It's of the belief that everyone has their bad days and we must understand and adjust accordingly. Okay, fine. But what about the entrenched issues, addictions, anger, etc., that surface or become exacerbated as the relationship takes its course? No one ever told us how to deal with this. It's a given that people put their best foot forward initially. That's whom we fall in love with, the fantasy person. When the evil twin has its day, it can be jolting. The rationale is that it's probably an isolated incident—until it isn't. Then what? There's a whole generation of put up and shut up out there. They may swear by tradition and have good reason to do so, but undoubtedly there were many disappointments and frustrations that accompanied the *Leave it to Beaver* façade. It's sad to think of the less-than-lived lives due to the constraints of the day. Structure is a key factor of functionality, but fear, humiliation, and embarrassment probably ruled the roost more often than not.

Our emotions play a huge part in how we deal with I Do and the fidelity factor. Raw emotion is a profound thing. There is no thought, just pure unrestrained reaction. We are hard-pressed to tame emotions without becoming a robotic nonentity. Emotions leak, jump, and burst out of us at any given moment. They take us to the mat before they can be rationally processed. A scent, a sound, a sight—a cottage cheese commercial can make us cry. Emotions overtake us with laughter, anger, envy, lust, joy. They're amazing attributes and can also be our worst enemy when unchecked. They have the capability to be a very dangerous element when fidelity has been kicked to the curb. *Fatal Attraction*, anyone?

Hope, on the other hand, can provide shelter from the storm. Hope is a valuable tool, but it must be handled judiciously. It is a positive trait and deserves to be generously served up and doled out in an affirming environment. It's best not to burden hope with unrealistic expectations. It can't perform maximally under those circumstances. Hope can't provide comfort if its true nature is misappropriated or false. It cannot be the catalyst for a situation that requires more concentrated modes of treatment.

Needless to say, there's a lot of emotion and hope that go into saying I Do. These tiny words are hardly big enough to hide behind, yet I'd venture to conservatively guestimate that 60 percent of those who say I Do actually mean:

I Do believe I can make this work even though I'm not in love.

I Do think I better marry before my biological clock stops ticking.

I Do want to be married now that I've hooked a sugar daddy/mama.

I Do hope my parents will be happy that I'm marrying the person of *their* dreams.

I Do feel I've made a mistake.

I Do love him/her but I doubt this will last.

I Do wish I would have called off the wedding.

I Do know I can get a divorce if it doesn't work out.

I Do not want to be here...

To tag onto the above, I do hope you contemplate this. There's a lot of role-playing and keeping up appearances for the sake of a dishonest union. This is serious business. This is your life. The one you get to live. What a privilege, you get to live a life! Choose to live it wisely and well. If you have the foresight to build it on a solid foundation while eliminating the common loop-holes, it will be markedly more enjoyable and meaningful.

It's understood that pressures and expectations can take their toll on a committed relationship. But guess what? If you're going to do this, it's your responsibility to put your big pants on and create a world with your mate that's equitable and workable in order to see I Do through. Which ever way you decide to divvy up the domestic roles is up to *both* of you. It's a format that is conceived by you, the couple. By all means incorporate outside influences and guidelines if they're an added benefit to your lives, but stay away if there are stressors that cannot be compromised. Be clear and upfront about that. These are not subjects best left to chance after walking down the aisle. Otherwise, you'll likely find yourself drowning in the statistics pool.

There are a million scenarios on how to create a working partnership. It is not one size fits all. That's where a lot of folks get tripped up. They think they have to lead their lives according to rules set by others. How your grandparents conducted their relationship has no real bearing on how you will conduct yours. If grandma and grandpa had a loving union, sure, take the good from that. Apply all the positive attributes, but if grandma was cooking over a hot stove all day and grandpa was out in the fields bringing home the bacon, that's not going to transfer if your lifestyle is worlds apart.

Ultimately, it's what is conducive to your personal relationship. Disclaimer: This doesn't speak to those who choose to live extreme lifestyles that may be outside the bounds of the law and recognized common decency. This speaks to the other 99.99 percent. To continue—maybe you do take on the historically established roles, one works outside the home, one works inside the home. Maybe both parties work and equally divide the chores at home. Maybe you're both too busy with work to concentrate much on the inside; hire a housekeeper, babysitter, call on family members, etc. If one has a business, then the other helps keep it organized. Point being, it's mix and match, heavy on the match. Make it so no one feels put upon and undervalued. Otherwise, this can be a starting point for potential transgressions.

Those who have lived together before saying I Do have already taken steps toward defining their roles within their relationship. Some would argue this is not the proper way to go about committing. Everyone is entitled to their opinion, but this isn't about slings and arrows. It would seem those who do set up household prior to matrimony have a better understanding of what to expect. This is not a guarantee the relationship will have longevity, but it is a jump-start toward adjusting to each other. There is also the contention that if vows aren't taken in the customary sense, it's far too easy to pack up and leave i.e., a continual cycle of committing, yet not fully committing; it's a valid point. But there are also couples that hold themselves up to the highest standards of commitment while supposedly living in sin, who last longer than those who have taken the trip down the gangway. As a reminder, the divorce rate is still a sticking point no matter what side of the traditional, non-traditional road you travel. There's still something rotten in the state of Denmark.

Those who haven't shared a roof prior to saying I Do may find themselves with an idealized concept. By the way, this isn't about advocating for either side, but rather taking a look from each standpoint. How is one to know if their mate is less than consistent when it comes to taking out the funky, smelly trash? How are you to know your mate likes to take three showers a day and you're the one left to deal with too many wet towels hanging over the shower stall? Or that he/she likes to wake up at 3 a.m. to do P90X? And this is the fairly innocuous stuff. Can you imagine when you're faced with something indisputably distasteful? Where's your family, clergy, friend, then? How do you even broach these subjects? Chances are you won't. It'll be too uncomfortable, awkward, or seemingly weird. You won't want anyone to know you have such a situation on your hands, and they certainly don't teach us about this—anywhere. Yes, some things are easily negotiated, but others do require help. As in, "Help! I had no friggin' clue—get me the heck outta here!"

As you can see, I Do is a little more than just showing up in your party frock. It's a whole lot more. We enable the disconnect by not thoroughly addressing the unquestionable meaning of commitment. If we continue to turn a blind eye, we will continue to see fidelity interrupted. We will continue to see statistics that reflect the decline of the marital institution. This isn't about promoting marriage one way or the other, but this is about advocating a more open and sound approach *before* a commitment is made, in order to avoid the hazards. Some suitable education beforehand does exist, but it's evident we have to revamp and reiterate the lesson plan. There's still an expansive void between the fantasy and "I-didn't-sign-up-for-this!"

In all fairness, we as a society have made great strides as far as acknowledging harmful issues that can hamper committed relationships. We know more about stress, disorders, abuse, domestic violence, etc. These issues were not as readily discussed in earlier generations as they are now. Thankfully we've come this far. But, we have to build even more awareness about the simple fundamental items. The all-important building blocks that can alleviate the initial conflicts that contribute to the breakdown of relationships.

Personally, I went through a confusing time during my marriage and sought counsel. I told the therapist some of my concerns, which I can't recall, but they were troubling at the time. They weren't make-or-break issues, but they were things that I wasn't sure how to handle, nor did I understand why some of these things were even happening. My therapist actually chuckled and said, "You seem genuinely surprised." I said, "I am. No one told me about this!" Thereafter I started sharing some of my inter-marital experiences with friends and family. I *needed* to chat about it. I had to figure some stuff out, and, of course—I was genuinely surprised. I wanted to understand what I was missing, if in fact I was. Turns out I had to talk a lot before anyone offered me their stories. A very telling and interesting observation, as this was my close circle! My guess is that people want to safeguard the sanctity of their world, but half the time it's about keeping your mouth shut for fear of others finding out that your life is not as groovy as you'd like everyone to believe.

One friend told me her husband once got so mad he threw a chair at the wall. Is that normal behavior? If so, why? What makes it acceptable? I understand we are all capable of flying off the handle, but do people commonly talk about these things or let them go? Do they play deaf and blind, then discuss the weather? I heard a few more stories—not normal. Granted, normal is relative, but some of what I heard erred way the heck on the other side, and I happen to err on the side of tolerance. Occurrences of this type, if not dealt with effectively, can lead once-caring partners into the recesses of infidelity.

Hopefully, incidences of this sort are being handled with care. I have my doubts. But then again who knows, because no one *continues* to talk about resolving these alarming issues. Well, it's time we do.

Chapter 3

Pretty Rose-colored Glasses

So you've done it. You've found someone who loves and adores you. You're snugly ensconced in your favored way of life. You may or may not be married or living under the same roof, but you do in fact have a mate. This person has agreed to have a committed relationship with you and you with him/her. Up close and personal with fidelity. You've left your days of playing and straying behind you. Hallelujah! You've been saved! What a relief to be out of the single scene. How many more bars, dates, and getting-to-know-yous can one possibly endure? You're ready to settle down and check out this version of bliss. Here's a grab bag of examples.

First up: two people who live apart but who have had the "talk." You are mine, I am yours, we are one. You are a devoted couple. You've put your time in getting to know one another and you're confident you want to share strictly amongst yourselves. You have joined the hallowed ranks of coupledom. No one is waiting around for the next one to make a move. Should you call or wait for him/her to? Are you being too needy if you call first? Heck, no, you've now graduated to chatting a few times a day. You don't have to wait until the default designated timeframe (during lunch, after work, etc.). You can pick up the dang phone any old time just to say hello. You don't even need that person to answer. It doesn't matter because you have earned the right to dial at will.

You start booking in advance to see each other. You *know* you'll be seeing each other. No more wondering if so-and-so will ask you out for a date this coming weekend. Nope. You're the only date going. You'll be spending weekends and a few evenings during the week at each other's place. If everything goes according to plan, you'll get a key. You'll be able to drop on by his/her place whenever. No one needs to be home. It will be enough to be in your other half's world. Snuggle on the couch. Grab something from the fridge; familiarity starts to build. Everything's coming up roses and daffodils.

Okay, let's proceed to scenario two: the cohabiters. These two have taken their relationship to the next level. They haven't quite made it to the altar, but they are living under the same pitched roof. A testing ground of sorts. They are setting up shop as a preliminary measure. Maybe not your mama's relationship, but it's a more often than not an accepted commonplace occurrence. These two, depending: share rent, split the utility bills, alternate buying groceries, etc. and are probably responsible for whatever individual bills they have brought to the table. This is a generalization, of course. Couples set their own ground rules, but we'll go with this for now. Before they even cross the threshold to their new abode, they have to take stock of their personal belongings and how to incorporate them. Downsizing a tad here, splurging for new acquisitions to suit the new dwelling, there. The meshing of two distinct households is a bit of an ordeal. Chances are they have adorned their own personal space to reflect their own individual taste. It's not likely it will be an exact match when intermingled. Not a problem. Love bridges these gaps and it's a good excuse to buy brand-new things to accommodate both parties. Creating *your* space is the objective. Will a ring and a promise of forever be an acquirement as well? Not sure. It's a feasible prospect perhaps, but for now this works fine. They're just happy to be in each other's company day in and day out. Hey, how about a dog?

Scenario three: engaged. This couple may or may not be living together. If cohabitating, they're good to go. They've already established their adaptation of domesticity and just need to make it official. If not, they more than likely are sharing as much time as possible together while trying to cement their future plans. Either way, their nuptials are on the horizon. They are deep in before-thee-major-commitment stage. Venues, dresses, tuxedos, food, flowers, seating charts, etcetera times ten. The excitement fuels the momentum. The flushed, blushing soon-to-be bride and her proud, smiling-somewhat-nervous groom are caught up in the pre-connubial vortex. Family and friends are giddy with anticipation. The dog and cat just want to know what's for dinner.

We have three different common scenarios. Not unlike one would find in the real world. Maybe not unlike a situation you currently find yourself. All seem to be pleased with their choices. All seem to be leading in a hopeful direction. We're told this is the order of things. Once the intent is in place, the rest will follow, right?

A revisit of scenario one…

Tony and Cleo have established a fantastic rhythm for their liaison. Cleo makes tasty homemade dinners at her place on Tuesdays and Thursdays. She loves cooking for her man.

Tony takes her out to eat at one of the local haunts in his neck of the woods on Wednesdays. Mondays and Fridays they usually spend apart. It's healthy to have some downtime until they fully establish themselves, a little breathing room. She's out meeting friends for that great happy hour around the corner, attending her yogilates class or at home perusing the latest, greatest cookbook. He's throwing back specialty brews with the boys, playing in his Tuesday night baseball league, or catching up on loose ends at work. Saturdays and Sundays are spent together at Tony's. Occasionally they're out and about on side trips. All good.

Some months into it Cleo starts to feel things are becoming stagnant. She's tired of cooking dinners and not doing much else with Tony during the week because of distance and work schedule. This routine is getting old and boring. Shouldn't Tony be talking about maybe moving in together? Wouldn't it be easier if we consolidated everything instead of wasting time by schlepping 45 minutes in traffic? He never talks about a future.

Tony's still adjusting. He thinks Cleo needs to chill. She's calling a lot and not saying much of anything, but she's definitely giving him plenty of attitude. Annoying! He can't handle her right now. No more Sundays. He needs more personal space.

Cleo doesn't know why Tony doesn't get it. How can he not know what she's feeling? Tony knows how much she cares for him. It doesn't take a genius to figure out the next step. And now he says he can't see her on Sundays? Catching up on work? Are you kidding?! This really pisses her off. She initiates a girls' weekend. A looong weekend. Maybe he'll figure it out then.

Tony can finally breathe! He made an excuse not to see Cleo before she left. Didn't go over well, but, whatever. He's got time to do anything he wants. Tickets to the game, boys!

Cleo and the girls are dressed to kill. Who needs Tony?! Someone else will want to spend time with me. I am lookin' good. What? A drink for me? Salud!

Great teams. Good friends. Fine weather. No Cleo, no 'tude. Who needs it? Hel-looo…quite the seatmate. Share your peanuts? Thanks, don't mind if I do…

Cleo and Tony were soon happy to have Tuesday, Wednesday, Thursday, Saturday and Sunday again—just not with each other.

Scenario two resumed:

Jack and Jill are basking in their good fortune to have found each other. She's beautiful and remarkably easygoing. He's on the fast track with a prestigious job. They have an exciting life. They cruise the town, dine out, listen to music, attend events, do a little shimmy, shimmy here and there and make steamy love. Good times.

Soon, Jack notices Jill isn't very skilled in the domestic department, nor is she much for conversation. He cleans and cooks better than she can, and forget about discussing anything of substance. What's the deal? She lived on her own. You think she'd know the basics. Then again, she's gorgeous, great in bed, and doesn't nag. She's definitely his personal best. No big deal.

Funny, Jill didn't know Jack worked so hard. She welcomes his income and job perks, but didn't realize how much time he puts in. She's not used to being overlooked. I guess as long as he's climbing the ladder to improve *their* life, possibly permanently, it's worth it. No worries.

Jack can't believe Jill's messiness, or her inane chatter. How did he miss that? And her spaghetti is the worst ever. It's spaghetti! How can you screw that up?! He stops after work for some real food. He says he's putting in more hours, it's not a total lie.

Jill suggests a date night. Jack says he doesn't have time. He leaves early and arrives late. She offers to make him dinner, he says it's easier to eat out. She asks about his day, he doesn't want to talk. About what, her new lipstick shade?

Jill constantly pouts and whines that Jack's not around. He's found a million other places he'd rather be. She says they rarely have sex. Jack only wants sex based on need, not desire. She/he never thought he'd turn *her* down.

Is that alcohol on Jack's breath? Working late? Liar! Jill pleads and cries, but nothing works. Who does he think he is? Does he realize how many men she rejected to be with him? She deserves better!

Jack attends a work mixer. He's had a rough day, not to mention the crap going on at home. He's feeling tired and unloved. Along comes sexy Sadie—and… Jack fell down and broke his crown. Jill called a plumber to remove the piles of pasta from her clogged drain. Hmm…plumbers make pretty good money. Luckily he's also handy with squeaky mattress springs. And Jill came tumbling after.

Scenario three further explored:

Anastasia and William live in a home that is immaculate and stylish. Anastasia brings in the bucks and has spared no expense in creating her version of a comfortable life. William is in awe of Anastasia and eagerly follows her lead. Anastasia finds William to be a suitable match. William is thrilled to be in her orbit. They are contentedly anticipating their fast-approaching wedding.

Anastasia has planned for her big day since she was five. She wants the princess ceremony—and she will get it. She invests without restraint for her life-long dream. She has her finger in every pie, a voice in every matter. Nothing is left to error.

William usually backs away when Anastasia is in mission control mode. Occasionally she makes amends with a fun trip or a great gift, but that's not enough. William wants to stand on his own. He wants to help. Isn't it *their* wedding? Anastasia waves him off and says not to worry.

William *is* worried. He's getting the full-blown version of who she can be and he's not liking it. Anastasia can't be sidetracked with minor tensions. A fairy-tale wedding is in her future. William has always been there. He always will be. Now, fondant or buttercream for the cake?

William needs to talk. Anastasia is fervently planning a gala. She's busy, can't you see? Just go with the flow. And William does—go. He leaves a note. Anastasia doesn't notice. She scarcely notices William isn't home from work until hours later. Odd, he's not answering his phone. Maybe he's out with friends to relieve some stress. Stress? What stress? He hasn't done anything! Oh, a note…Note to self: cancel happily-ever-after.

These couples started out with noble objectives. All probably wanted to achieve a positive end goal, but unfortunately each and every one fell short. Do you see where they went wrong? Do you recognize where other choices could have been made to propel them along a more constructive path? Can you identify options that would have prevented them from turning away from their loved one?

Example one: Cleo wanted to get to the next level. Tony wanted to level out. Cleo expected Tony to know her desires. Tony can't read minds, or between the lines. Cleo pushed her right intentions in the wrong way. Tony in turn pulled back due to her projected disappointments. They both decided rocking the boat was easier than speaking their piece. Neither one bothered to sit and talk about what they were truthfully feeling about each other, and themselves. No one wanted to deal. They each acted out, gave up, and gave in to their base desires due to a misunderstanding of the situation and pent-up frustration.

Example two: Jack was blind to Jill's shortcomings. He solely focused on her physical traits. Jill lived by her looks and didn't bother to hone essential skills. Jack needed more. Jill just needed Jack. Jack wanted a decent meal. Jill wanted her meal ticket. Jack was an easy, solid, financial catch. Jill was merely a sparkly, shiny trophy. Sex was their only common ground and even that waned. They both exhibited a superficial, immature, and stereotypical view of what constitutes a relationship. This was also coupled with lack of emotional depth and not effectively voicing their dissatisfaction.

Example three: Anastasia developed her assertive skills without much thought to her people skills. William, unskilled, allowed her controlling behavior. Anastasia wanted to live her fantasy. William thought Anastasia was his. Anastasia was self-centered and driven. William was submissive and easily pacified. One was over-valued, the other, under-valued. Instead of acknowledging their polar differences and working with the strengths and weaknesses of each to their gain, they dismissed and alienated each other. Resentments easily build under these circumstances. Material things are substandard replacements for self-esteem and being cared for. In this type of dysfunctional atmosphere the internal void in both continually struggles to be filled.

To those couples that have been married many years, a portion of the aforementioned settings also apply to them. They've just chosen to remain in the relationship and stay distracted with family duties, work, and home. Too much time invested in the comfort zone to budge. Can't quite get up the energy to alter the dynamics or leave the marriage. Complacency and a measure of fear have set up permanent residence in the household. Where would I go? The kids have their own families and lives. Who will want me at this age? What will I do? I have no real place in the modern world. Here's a thought: buy a new pair of sneakers, do a few hops in place, embark on long walks, break a sweat here and there, and then start jumping over those hurdles. Take stock of your assets, the greatest of which is your mind-set, and work them to your advantage.

Do you identify with any of these paradigms? Rose-colored glasses a little smudged? If so, you might want to take a second, third, or fourth glance. After all, it's to your benefit to make sure you look both ways before you cross...the line.

Chapter 4

Survey Says!

In this chapter you will find answers to a survey that asked four simple questions:

1. **What are your thoughts about infidelity while married?**
2. **Why do you think women cheat while married?**
3. **Why do you think men cheat while married?**
4. **Should there be accountability for infidelity while married—if caught?**

I wanted to see what the opinions were in regards to pushing the bounds of fidelity (please note: there has been a time lapse but the gist remains the same). Gender is the only qualifier. However I did include one vocation, as it offers an added merit for this purpose. Seven men and seven women volunteered their answers. It reads in male–female order.

Male –

What are your thoughts about infidelity while married?

In answer to a similar question in a recent interview, this is what Melanie Griffith said: "I would feel so hurt (if Antonio were cheating on me). I don't know if humans were meant to be with only one person. I don't think so. But I don't believe Antonio could tolerate my being with someone else. Just as I couldn't tolerate his being with someone else."

Irrespective of what one is able to tolerate or not, the fact remains: the humans are not made to be only with one person. Marriage is based on "till death do us part," and yet recognizing impossibility of that vow, we as a society have basically accepted divorce and serial monogamy. The remaining taboo is now "cheating while married." And when talking of marriage, you cannot possibly single out sexual fidelity and not hundreds of other factors that keep marriages glued together or tear them apart. Now we are treading the waters of exclusivity in possessing our partner's body and soul. But when we talk about fidelity, we are only talking about the body, why? Only the sexual fidelity does not make for a lasting and happy marriage. In my opinion, this business of expecting fidelity in marriage is overrated.

Why do you think women cheat while married?

I find the accusation "cheating" offensive. But for the simplicity's sake I will live with the general connotation of what cheating is all about. The biggest reason men and women cheat on each other is that they are suddenly attracted to someone else. When the attraction overwhelms them beyond control and beyond reason, they are pulled to that other person like two magnets. Mind you, this attraction has nothing to do with no longer being attracted to one's respective spouse or to the couple having relationship problems in general. Just that, it is so natural to be attracted to someone else and still be in love with the one you're married to or are already in love with.

One of the reasons women find to justify their straying is if they know or suspect that their men is cheating on her and her doing the same, means getting even. It's easier to blame than to accept the blame. Or the fact she has just fallen out of love or in love with someone else.

Why do you think men cheat while married?

Neither for men nor for women, cheating, is not something that is done pre-meditated. Like I mentioned above, the most compelling reason would be an intense attraction. It's also in men's nature to hunt and capture, especially if the woman he is attracted to is hard to get. And as even the '70s German/Argentine feminist Esther Villar realised, as woman is a manipulative animal, men is polygamous—the facts that if understood and accepted could make life so much easier.

When two people say their vows, neither of them is plotting an eventual cheating scenario as plan B. It's something that happens. They don't do it to hurt the other. But the way the society has set up the expectations, the real cheating happens are the lies with which they try to cover their tracks.

Should there be accountability for infidelity while married—if caught?

This question makes me laugh. Should there be a law to lock up the partner—if caught red handed with someone else? There are enough laws about that if it becomes main reason for a divorce. In the meanwhile, both partners would have probably suffered enough emotional turmoil to yet subject them to "accountability," whatever that means.

Female –

1. Infidelity while married is just wrong. The marriage commitment is about two people committing to each other.

2. Women who cheat while married are probably just looking for that extra attention.

3. Men who cheat while married are probably just looking for that extra attention.

4. Yes, accountability should be had. Is it really worth it? Probably breaking your marriage, I doubt it.

Male – (priest)

Since I'm on the outside looking in I'm not sure if I'm qualified to opine on the subject. It looks like a lose-lose situation for me, but I'll bite:

1. Bad idea

2. Loneliness, lack of attention/affection, revenge (he cheated first)

3. Hormones

4. There is always accountability caught or not caught. You either pay now or later. On the other hand, I always advise

a cheating spouse that if they have really ended it and the other spouse has no way of knowing about it, leave it alone. However, most spouses know something's up, regardless of how cleverly you cover your tracks (except for Herman Cain, it seems).

Female –

1. I think it happens a lot, even when it is not happening, spouses can dwell on it and be very suspicious of each other. I don't think it has to kill a relationship, but bringing another person into the couple's lives usually stirs up lots of hurt feelings and mistrust. For me, it is a forgivable offense but not something that I can accept often because I do feel very betrayed by it.

2. I think that women more often cheat because they are not getting what they need emotionally out of their marriage. Maybe some also do it because they are bored and they meet someone exciting. Others may do it out of revenge if their husband cheated.

3. Some men feel trapped by marriage and an affair can make them feel like they are free. Some men may also do it because it makes them feel like more of a "man" if they are feeling insecure in other areas of their lives. I think men also are much more likely to take an opportunity that presents itself without thinking about how it would affect their spouse. They may consider it something that doesn't have anything to do with their spouse.

4. Accountability - if caught?
I don't know. I think the couple needs to really talk about

it and learn to trust each other again but if the relationship is to be healthy, they need to move on and not let this be something that continues to be dwelt upon. Also, the person who did the cheating needs to be willing to talk about it and take responsibility for it. They need to make an effort to be with their partner and help them get through it.

Male –

1. Try to avoid it if possible.
2. Lonely.
3. Because we're MEN.
4. Yes.

Female –

1. I don't think it's good or what I would want if I were married.

2./3. I think both men and women cheat for the same reasons: not happy in their relationships, not feeling appreciated, not feeling appealing to your spouse. Sometimes it is the circumstance a person finds him/herself in that they did not plan on. Revenge.

4. This is a hard question for me to answer, each situation is different and I don't know the law when it comes to divorce and it has so much to do with emotions and how far do you go back to what was said and done to one another.

Male –

As to adultery, 7 billion people can't be wrong, can they?

Female –

1. I believe that infidelity in marriage is wrong. However, that is not to say that in some circumstances it can't be worked out depending on the intent of the person. In other words, a lapse in judgement as opposed to repeat behavior.

2. I believe women cheat when they are either feeling very neglected or unhappy in a marriage. Also, if they really fall in love.

3. On the contrary I believe most men will cheat given the opportunity and if they think they can get away with it—has nothing to do with being unhappy or falling in love

4. Yes, I believe that the cheating party should have to pay in a monetary sense. They are breaking a contract and all contracts have provisions when broken. While you can never compensate for the emotional hurt, people may think twice before cheating if they know there are consequences to pay.

Male –

1. Monogamy is a manufactured idea to serve the state in producing soldiers and taxpayers. But it's fine if it works for you. Some lucky couples are true life partners and that's probably as blessed a state as can be! Life requires experimentation as sex is a huge learning experience. To

avoid extra-marital relationships because the church says so just means you'll sneak. Wives don't want husbands to "cheat" because they may lose his financial support.

2. Because it's too tempting and fun and usually because they are dissatisfied and feel trapped in this artificially created state of monogamy. Also, they may find sex within marriage too same-old, same-old. The passion is gone.

3. Same as above with the addition that married women too frequently stop having sex so the husbands are stuck and resentful. Women are designed to use sex for security and babies. Very few women really continue to want sex afterwards unless they need to re-entrap a man or they're very much their own person—in control of themselves, not in reaction mode, and passionate about their lives, which carries over to their sex lives. This is a huge generalization, of course, but I believe it is more often true than not.

4. If a partner "cheats" it would be best if an open discussion should occur between the partners to understand why it needed to happen and then both make changes to improve or dissolve the marriage. My first big relationship was an "open" one. It was the '70s! It worked and rarely did either of us find the satisfaction in our one-night stands that we did together so we always came back. As long as it was about equal and the "other person" was not too threateningly rich or beautiful, we always were fine. When we broke up it had nothing to do with others, only ourselves.

I have cheated twice when I was in a resentful state about my wife's constant refusal. I felt great afterwards: invigorated and revalidated as a man. I wouldn't ever tell because wives have legal power over husbands and beware a woman scorned. In former relationships, on two occasions I had an opportunity to cheat but didn't do it because the relationships were strong and I preferred not to mess around. Ideally, sex would be guilt-free and people could do as they wish without bonds and boundaries. This would be more natural, but in our present world where we all feel so fragile and lacking, it would be difficult to have open relationships without problems.

Female –

1. I think that men and women are similar with respect to why they would cheat, and I think there are many reasons why people cheat:

a. Some people don't believe in monogamy. They may be open about this or they may secretly not believe in monogamy, but not want to tell their spouse because either their spouse would leave them or they don't want their spouse to have "outside options" or both. These people believe that there is nothing wrong with having outside sexual activity—that's it's "more natural" than monogamy and generally believe "nobody gets hurt if nobody knows." These people likely still see their spouse as their primary significant emotional relationship and the outside activities as "just sex."

b. Some people are just pretty selfish and narcissistic and just want to do whatever they want because they care more about what they want than their partner's feelings. (These people are the prototypical "cad" types.)

c. Some people have personal issues or marriage issues that they do not or cannot deal with squarely so they seek an "escape" in another relationship or person. They are essentially running away from facing problems with a distraction/fantasy that will never become a reality because they are using it as a fantasy escape. These would be the types who have long-term affairs but never actually divorce their spouse. I think the "other woman" or "other man" are complicit because they for some reason are also afraid of having a real relationship, so a married man or woman is less threatening. Either that, or the "other man/ woman" craves attention and affection so much that they don't care that the cheater is bullshitting them.

d. Some people just fail to keep the emotional intimacy alive in their marriage and their feelings/attraction fizzles out. In these cases, spouses are not connected to one another and they are just going through the motions. Interest in someone else inevitably occurs and is a signal to them that they need to make changes, or to end their marriage, or they resort to item c (above).

e. I think sometimes people just do stupid things in the moment that they never thought they would do—i.e., they flirt a little or allow someone to kiss them—because of an unusual context, mood, or mental state. If it is just something stupid that they don't really want, they will "snap out of it" before going too far, get themselves out of the situation, feel bad about it, and vow to themselves that they will never do it again. (They may 'fess up to the spouse and express great remorse.)

4. Should there be accountability for infidelity while married—if caught? YES, trust has to be re-established. Trust is needed as a foundation in a relationship. If infidelity occurs, there needs to be a discussion of why it occurred, how it affects the other spouse, and what needs to be done to repair the relationship or address problems. Everybody needs

to be clear about what they need and what they expect from the other partner. It is not fair to put on a charade. If it is one stupid small and uninvolved mistake (item e) maybe it would be okay not to tell the spouse because the cheater feels bad and has learned his lesson, and the pain and mistrust the other spouse would feel is unnecessary. However, if it is anything more involved, it probably indicates deeper problems that the couple has to solve together. Without that how can each member re-invest in the relationship? If you mean should you tell someone that their spouse is cheating, that is trickier. I think that I would generally confront the cheater about what is going on and encourage him/her to come clean to their spouse on their own terms or make needed changes (dump the affair). Whether or not you tell the spouse who was cheated depends on the person and your relationship with him/her. I personally would want someone to tell me if I was being cheated on, but different people would have a different preference.

Male –

Infidelity is a heavy subject and has a lot of complications. We have made it more complicated with our modern society and various life-styles. I know for me the answers to these issues have changed in light of what I am involved with, and my life experiences at the time. Ultimately I think that what works best is the traditional roles of a traditional marriage. However that has not been my life experience.

Ultimately two people who completely commit to each other no matter what, each looks out for the best for each other and not self. Unfaithfulness comes from, at least in part, putting oneself above the mate. People cheat for many reasons...many are not really good ones and we usually find ways to justify the act, if nothing else, in our minds. People can, and do, deal with this issue in many ways and find ways to get over infidelity, or forgive it, or whatever. It does and will happen...but not in all situations, and can happen and not repeat. We make it what it is.

From a "it meant nothing and was a fling of the moment" and "it would not happen again" or "it was meaningless." Like all the other situations when something presents itself, what happens happens. There's something lacking in the relationship like no respect, or not enough money, or whatever the issue is, including unsatisfactory sex in the marriage. Likely sex is just part of the problem and there are many other issues around it. Those other issues also need to be resolved or the infidelity thing is a symptom, not the illness.

Female –

My thoughts about infidelity whilst married are that it is wrong. No matter what the problems are that a couple are encountering whilst they are married, it is always better to communicate the problems. Obviously this may be difficult for couples, but in the long run if a couple can't talk with each other then they lose the chance of building a longstanding relationship. Women may cheat for a number of reasons: the bog standard* one is, the husband is working all the time then has no time for his wife. Or, he may no longer want sex and if she has a higher sex drive then this may be another factor why she cheats.

Men may cheat for a number of reasons: bog standard* one, he has met someone at work, she is young, attractive, and she pays him lots of compliments, more than he gets at home. Or, another factor, he is working away from home a lot, and he again gets the attention from a number of females. The man may also cheat if he has a higher sex drive than his wife. She is too tired either from work, children, or that she just plain does not want to have sex all the time. This may be another factor why the man cheats.

Male –

1. What are your thoughts about infidelity while married? I have no real thoughts about it, I believe this is a personal issue between the parties that are married and do not involve society.

2. Why do you think women cheat while married? Not getting what they want in their marriage, and this stands for the men, to answer question 3.

3. Why do you think men cheat while married? Same as above.

4. Should there be accountability for infidelity while married—if caught? I feel the accompanying shame and dismantling of the marriage is enough that fall on the participants.

---

*Bog standard: British informal phrase meaning completely ordinary or unremarkable.

Female –

1. I think it is a (common) symptom of one of two things really…a marriage that is going through a lot of stress, and/or problems whereby the two people don't feel so very connected (either physically or emotionally) at that moment, or, it is a sign or symptom of someone who is not and possibly never has placed fidelity as a high value in the relationship. So my position is to look at what the infidelity is a SIGN OF, and if any reconciliation is to be made, that looking at the underlying reasons will be the core of what is targeted, in order for change to occur. Until those issues are addressed, then a reconciliation cannot occur. Usually, this is enough to break a marriage and reconciliation does not happen. Those who are able to reconcile and go on, often have an improved relationship, but this is rare.

2. Because women basically get the majority of their emotional needs met in their relationships, and the relationship with their spouse is that "main relationship." When women feel that their emotional (or sexual) needs are not being met by way of their husbands, some women will get those needs met elsewhere, but they may be less apt to seek it out. Oftentimes, it comes upon them: i.e., the man approaches that woman, (because men are often on the "hunt") and when that woman is vulnerable, in that those needs that I mentioned, are not being met, she is more likely to succumb to those advances of those men who are coming on to her. Or, she will "turn to a friend" for an emotional shoulder to cry on. Then, she will find herself in a position of being in an affair.

3. In many ways, same answer as above, the only difference in that men primarily get their "needs met" by way of their jobs/careers, and less so by way of relationships. But in the

case of men, since they tend to be more sexually driven, they are the ones seeking the woman out. In many other instances though it's simply because men are used to "the hunt" and they never fully acclimated to the idea that marriage would represent complete monogamy. They (men) seem to have a hard time accepting the fact that they will never ever be able to have other women sexually. I think in general, men just have a harder time at long-term monogamy.

4. Accountability to whom?

—

So, there you have it, or at least some of it. There are no true right or wrong answers. But as you can see, these are defined and diverse. What are yours?

Chapter 5

A Couple of True Tales

Here you'll find personal stories from a woman and man who have had encounters with the other side of fidelity. Glean from them what you can. Who knows, you may even recognize yourself.

Her story—I married at 21 years old the first time around. We were both young and heavily in lust. Hormones and immaturity were on overdrive. That marriage ended due to the fact my husband cheated on me. I imagine the gloss of having sex with me had worn off. His cheating affected me adversely. I seemed to have misplaced that recollection when I proceeded to do the same to someone else.

I was 34 years old when I married the second time. My husband adored me completely. I saw pure love in his eyes. We also shared a deep friendship. We were married for three years. Two years into the marriage is when I took a turn in another direction. There always seemed to be something off in the marriage, but I couldn't really place it, nor did I have the tools to communicate effectively or consider the issues on another level. For all intents and purposes, I thought my marriage was fine. But, I didn't have much to compare it to. No one ever taught or spoke to me about marriage in real-life terms. It was something that was supposed to be done. So, I did. Three times. I'm happy to say, the third one is sticking.

My second husband did not like to kiss. I loved kissing and I missed it. We had a regular sex life, but I was never truly satisfied. He was fine with it, although it seems he preferred masturbation, with or without me. He left evidence of this in a very open way. I always thought this wasn't quite right but that's about as far as it went. I never discussed it with him, or anyone else. There were other incidents that left me puzzled as well. I remember one time we went out with a few friends for drinks at a gay bar. Some men at the bar were flirting with my husband. Not a problem, except he blushed and started flirting back rather than saying he was there with his wife, etc. It was confusing and I didn't understand it. This was also 20 years ago when much wasn't discussed in that way, so we never spoke about it. Another problem for me was that my husband was boring. He was a kind, caring man but he never wanted to go out or do anything remotely exciting. He was always home, whereas my first husband was never home (too busy cheating). This husband was very much a homebody and liked it that way. Another issue was that he also lacked communication skills. I attribute that to the relationship he had with his father. It was contentious at best. In essence, we were two people in the unfortunate position of being without the benefit of real communiqué.

After a time I began questioning my husband's sexuality and all else that made me uncomfortable or unhappy. That is what allowed for my indiscretion. One evening after work I had gone out with co-workers for a drink or two. They were all familiar people to me, but I started to take more notice of one of the men (I use that word loosely, as he was only 21 years old). He was so different from my husband. First of all, he was 15 years my junior. He had long flowing hair (my husband was balding) and he dressed young and hip. We were both feeling the effects of alcohol and started flirting heavily. Soon thereafter we walked out to my car in the parking lot and started kissing like crazy. Man, did it feel good. Finally I'm kissing, really kissing! It was fantastic! It was exciting, erotic, and fun. It didn't take long for us to get into my car and have sex. It was intoxicating, animal sex. At last! I never had this with my husband. For a brief moment I thought, WTF have I done? But there was no stopping me. The vows were now broken and I was going for it. I was mesmerized.

The affair began in earnest from that point on. I would tell my husband that I was going out with friends to concerts, gatherings, etc. My lover and I would have lunchtime quickies in my car or at a friend's house. I was caught up in the idea of having unbridled chemistry. The fact that it was wrong was also a part of the attraction. I was being selfish, but I didn't care. I rejected my husband sexually and resented his place in my life. I would actually go home with the smell of sex on me and didn't give it a second thought.

After a time my husband did start to suspect. He started calling my cell phone and would ask, "Where are you?" Interestingly enough, he never asked who I was with. One evening my illicit partner called my home while drunk. I picked up, and unbeknownst to me, so did my husband on the upstairs line. My partner started saying how much he missed me. I told him the same. When we hung up my husband came down the stairs, sat on a step and asked if I was having an affair. I told him, no, it was just a kid who had a crush on me. Then the fighting began. He asked who he was. I told him he was someone I met through a friend. Then, finally, yes—I was having an affair. He told me to move out. I obviously wanted out.

I asked a friend to help me move while my husband was at work. My husband didn't know which day I'd be moving. I did think about him briefly, having to go home to a half-empty house, but I had already rented an apartment and was excited about my freedom and new life. I felt reborn, elated! No answering to anyone. I was completely self-absorbed in my own world. When he found out I had actually left, he broke down and cried. He told me he wanted to give it another try, but I had absolutely made my decision. I was very removed emotionally. No compassion. I had only one prevailing thought; get out and stay out.

The affair lasted 7–8 months. I had no real communication with my husband during this time. I still didn't consider his feelings. His lawyer contacted me, but that was about it. My partner and I were busy playing house (he was always with me, although not permanently). He was in love and I was only concerned about having a great time and living life on my own terms. That worked for a while. However, some of the after-effects were starting to build. I began to separate myself from my friends. I was embarrassed and "didn't want to hear about it" from anyone. I wanted to continue what I was doing without dealing with outside influences. Nonetheless, the inside influences were also starting to wear on me. The age difference between my partner and I was becoming more apparent. His friends would say, "She's too old." Believe it or not, it was hurtful. Although the sex was still great, everything started to take its toll.

Throughout this time, I was very much into exercise and met a man (15 years my senior, from one extreme to the other!) at the gym. We started to build a rapport. I gave him my number and he eventually called. I wasn't home, but my partner happened to be at my place and answered the phone. The man asked, "Is your mother home?" Okay, it is somewhat funny, but it sure hit home. When I returned, my companion mentioned the odd phone call. I told him that I was interested in this person and I thought it was time we started dating others. He was deeply hurt, but I knew I didn't want to do to him what I had done to my ex-husband. Not another affair. There were tears and his profession of love, but it had to be done. I knew in the long run all would be okay. We had both fulfilled some sexual fantasy and other superficial needs, now it was time to move on.

I am now fifteen years into my third marriage (the man from the gym). We have had our fair share of trials and tribulations, but we have learned to examine ourselves and our behavior in order to work toward our common goals. I never speak to my first husband. My second husband and I have managed to come to reasonable terms with my wrongdoing, although we do not truly keep in contact. He has reached out, but I was either too embarrassed or didn't want to lead him on, so I didn't encourage communication. He still remains heterosexual to my knowledge. My young cohort is now married to a woman close to his age and has children.

In retrospect, what I've learned is this: I will never cheat on anyone again. I carried so much shame and humiliation stemming from my own behavior. I treated my ex-husband without a shred of dignity. I acted without regard toward another individual. Although I can't measure the depth of his pain, I can imagine, as I carried a great wound for having committed such an egocentric act. It's true the more you move away, the softer the memory becomes, yet the lasting effects are far-reaching. I humbly wish I had never been within its grasp.

His story—I was 38 years old and had been married for six years. By all accounts I was living the American Dream: successful business, a wife who I loved completely, two wonderful, healthy kids, a beautiful home, luxury cars and fantastic vacations. I was a busy, committed, mover and shaker. I wanted to continue to excel and make more money. I was Gap in my early married life, now I was Prada. I was doing well.

It was summer and I was looking forward to getting away to our seaside rental. My wife and kids were already at the vacation house. I was to meet them the following day. On the way home from work I stopped at a bar to wait out the traffic before heading home to pack. It was common for me to do so. I had a glass of wine as per usual. A glass of alcohol for me here and there was no big deal. I was a social drinker. This particular day I was contemplating my new business venture. My corporation had agreed to finance my franchise. Even though I was excited, I also felt the pressure. There was a good deal of money at stake and I had to prove myself in a different capacity. I was up for the challenge and change, but anxiety was starting to mount. I had my drink, left the bar and walked by a newsstand that caught my eye. There was a paper that advertised massages, etc. I was the type of person to get massages somewhat regularly, but this paper advertised "special" types of services. I can not effectively explain in the moment what I thought, but I did experience an adrenalin rush. I wanted to call one of the numbers. I wanted to make an appointment. I wanted to explore. And I did.

A Couple of True Tales

The woman on the phone said to meet her in an hour. I drove to the location early. There was a bar nearby, so I had a couple of beers to relieve my nerves. This type of service was unfamiliar territory for me and I didn't know what to expect other than the obvious. I went to the address and was greeted by an attractive woman. I took her lead as I didn't know this particular protocol. We exchanged benign greetings. She then proceeded to ask me a few questions (women in this industry use code questions), which I found out later was to assess whether or not I was a cop. I guess I passed the test because she asked me to put the $300 on the table. $300 for an hour. No money ever physically exchanged hands. She said to get undressed and we proceeded to get to the subject at hand—sex. After the deed was done, we chatted briefly. She told me about her kids. I understood this later to be an appeal for a tip. I was in and out of her place within 40 minutes. I went back to the bar for a drink…What had I just done?!!

On the ride home I was crushed by guilt, shame, and remorse. I was now in the category of "those" men; men of wealth who took on mistresses and prostitutes because their ego and money allowed them to. I had family members of this sort and actually admired them. I thought I was deserving of this too. I'd later find out what I was actually deserving of.

All kinds of thoughts were flooding my brain as I drove. I had no idea how I was going to handle this once in my wife's presence. While I was experiencing this internal combustion I noticed a small paper cut on my finger. I panicked. My finger had been *inside* that woman. Oh my god, I may have contracted AIDS! You have to understand this was back when the disease was still somewhat in its infancy. I thought my life was far too removed from the possibility of anything of this nature happening to *me*, but this was quite an eye opener.

One act of carnal pleasure had created myriads of negative backlash. I was scared shitless and literally shuddered. What if I give it to my wife? I have the potential to kill her! I know God is now looking at me like I'm the devil. I started creating scenarios in my head: I'll wear a condom with my wife (I never wear a condom with her). I'll tell her it's preventative measures for conception. We had a second child just a couple of years prior. We don't want to get pregnant again do we? She'll think I'm crazy. In that moment I was —

I wanted to see a doctor ASAP and went to the nearest emergency center. I needed to take an AIDS test—now! Admissions asked why I was there. I told them I may have AIDS. They said a doctor would be with me shortly. The doctor came and asked what was concerning me. I held up my pinky finger with the paper cut and told him, "I think I have AIDS!" He looked at it and said, "Oh, so this is what AIDS looks like." I understand how he may have found humor in it (funny, if you weren't me), but at the time I was a nervous wreck. I told him I wanted to take a test. Fine, done, but the results won't be back for a few weeks—an eternity.

The next morning I make my way to meet my wife and kids. Now what do I do?! I can't have intercourse with my wife if I have the potential to harm her. We're due to have a great week with the kids and friends. How the hell am I supposed to handle all this?! Also, how can I survive a few weeks of not knowing the test results? Once I arrive at the summer rental my wife takes one look at me and says, "You look terrible." I tell her work was stressful. She offers to talk about it—no, I'm fine. The kids greet me with happiness and laughter. I tell my wife every fifteen minutes that I love her. She asks me what's going on? I tell her I don't say those words enough.

Later that evening we manage to have a great dinner with friends. By the end of the day I was thoroughly exhausted.

Per habit, we put the kids to bed and retired to our bedroom. I don't know how I can *not* have sex with her. I'm feeling dirty. I need to tell her somehow. But instead of telling her the real truth, I make up a story about a massage getting out of hand. I positioned myself to be the victim. *I* was the one that had been aggressively pursued. I didn't mention the possibility of AIDS, only my carelessness. My wife cried and cried. She said I should have taken it to the grave with me. I should have kept the guilt to myself. And, of course, she didn't want to sleep with me. Ironically that worked in my favor. However, we had the rest of the week to endure. We put on a happy façade for the kids and friends and went about our business. At night we slept in the same room, she on the bed, me on the floor. All the while I'm numb.

When we returned to our home my wife decided we needed to stay together for the sake of the kids. I knew she still loved me and I realized how difficult this must be for her. She didn't ask me to leave. She wanted us to do the best we could. We decided to play it by ear. I eventually did find out my test was negative. Relief! We started our lovemaking once more. I vowed to myself to never do something like this again—at least for the next year and a half.

Work was heavy. I was drinking more to repress my emotions. My misconduct prior gave way to the onset of my unfavorable drinking habit. During this time I was also traveling frequently to meet clients. I needed a release from the stress. I needed an escape…I needed to start seeing prostitutes again, this time, whenever I felt the urge. I made sure I was meticulously discreet. I didn't tell anyone. I funneled the money spent through my various companies where it could never be tracked. As a rule, I chose women who didn't share the same hair color as my wife. I wore protection, and most importantly, I wasn't having an *actual* affair. I hadn't given my heart to anyone. I was well within the bounds of decency. Of course, this was a version of my own pathetic brand of respect, and also used to ward off guilt.

My motivators were risk, escape, and entitlement. The adrenalin rush of a fresh encounter kept me fueled. Escapism through unemotional sex, along with alcohol, were my essentials. My sense of entitlement ran long and wide. Hey, I was providing a very good life for my wife. She had pretty much everything she wanted. If she ever found out, how dare she even remotely question anything I do? She had no idea of the burdens I carried. She doesn't get it: leave me alone and get me a drink! She became bitchy along the way, giving me more reason to act out. She would complain to her friends, the country club set. They would carp and moan about how hard it was to raise kids, their husband's lack of attention, etc. Resentments escalated. I'd go home drunk and purposefully pick fights so she wouldn't want to have sex with me. I wanted raw sex, the kind that came without any kind of attachment whatsoever. I didn't want routine married sex. For me, no matter how you spiced it up, it became routine. There's an old adage, "You know what you pay prostitutes for?" – "To leave." Which is exactly what my wife asked me to do a month and a half later.

I was emotionally destroyed by her request, but I left. My children's welfare was of great concern. Initially we wanted to do the best by them. At some point, that also shifted. My life took on many unsettling forms thereafter. We were separated for three years before divorcing. A lot of complex emotions surfaced. All the usual stuff you hear about when undergoing this circumstance, but, I also had to address my own personal tumult which was separate and apart from my marriage.

Would I do it again? No. I was in an immature relationship. If I were to marry again, I'd choose a more mature and evolved woman. We were both in our mid-twenties. We had communication issues. I also promoted the superficial. I eventually had to come to terms with my ego responses. Since then I have gone through many a roller coaster ride because of the transgressions, and other areas of my life that I didn't know were distressing me. I lost love, most of my money, and painfully, my children at times. My actions during that particular period of my marriage were the totality of all the things that were eating at my soul. I can safely say I'm much healthier now and plan on staying the course.

—

These are intense, provocative stories. None of us would willingly invite their experiences into our lives. These two made some very expansive and expensive mistakes. Luckily they have chosen a more optimistic path for their future. It goes without saying that deep-rooted issues, which we may or may not be aware of, have weighty long-term effects in the way we handle our relationships. This is a serious factor when dealing with fidelity. Wouldn't it be liberating to have this assessed, and hopefully resolved, before the inevitable fall?

Chapter 6

I Don't

It's natural to feel irritants and frustrations within a union where fidelity is a key factor. You are, after all, completely different people with separate histories, experiences, and expectations. It's rare that people meet and instantly venture into a near-perfect alliance. Not impossible, but extremely rare. I personally am not aware of anyone who's had this occurrence, but I hear it exists. If you're one of these people, please offer up your thoughts and helpful hints. We'd be most obliged. As for some of the others…

They don't want to be in a committed relationship or marriage any longer. What started out as a well-spring of love, hopes, and dreams, has now run dry. They don't want to continue on the rutted road of ambiguity and discontent that they helped to create. It's far easier to rationalize a way out of confrontation, which conveniently leads to self-justification. A case for self-justification could be: you feel you have to do something you *think* is wrong in order to fully realize you *know* it's wrong, rather than the impulsive, opportunistic happenstance that other indiscretions can stem from. One is conscious or pre-meditated thought, the other is no thought whatsoever. Pick your poison.

It's starkly evident if you're not armed with a reasonable amount of information, can't gauge your ethics rationally, or have poor examples to cull from, there is likely to be trouble in paradise. Fidelity then becomes an enormous chore. The first signs of discomfort within the relationship, if not addressed appropriately, will continue to build and eventually lead people into self-defeating behavior. There are plenty of real-life paradigms exhibited in the public forum, as well as for our viewing pleasure on television. One would hope witnessing entanglements of this type would give one pause *before* acting out. Like one big, heavy finger on the pause button. Have you seen: *Cheaters*, *Wicked Attraction*, *Deadly Affairs*, et al? Wild stuff, all supposedly true. These are not your typical bad-movie-of-the-week scenarios. These are the real deal. Shock, disgrace, stalking, beatings, shootings, hit men, murder, body mutilations, STDs, illegitimate children, pregnant women offed, the young left to fend without parents because mom or dad are dead and the other is in jail for the rest of his/her life for homicide—the partial list. Insanity personified. That's a lot of commotion to undergo because you feel you couldn't pull up a chair and have a decent conversation with your mate to talk a few things out, or didn't have the wherewithal to walk away in a civil manner, or couldn't tackle your own inner demons. Shows keep cropping up like this because, sadly, there is no shortage of subject matter. *Cheaters* has been on the air for twelve seasons. Someone's making a lot of money off of human folly. How about getting scared straight, reclaiming your righteous self, and stop feeding into less deserving coffers? Programs of this nature may make for titillating TV, but it goes without saying it doesn't make for a quality life. And don't think it couldn't happen to you.

Those who don't want to deal with the overriding relationship annoyances find themselves in an especially precarious position. They are unhappy and unfulfilled in their committed relationship and choose to release those frustrations outside the margins of their bond. They find themselves sharing their time, which is already limited, with someone else who may or may not have the knowledge that they have a "forever" partner, and they don't want to cross back over that line. They'd rather explore their options before completely jumping ship. The immediate sense of freedom and relief overcomes any sort of logic, responsibility, or accountability. The fact is: you are never free from your own limitations until you recognize them, and even though the relief is palpable, it's temporary. If anything, the exact opposite could be the result. How much freedom will you have once you're found out and your income and possessions diminish? The respite you sought is somewhere out in the foggy distance. Real freedom is being able to resolve issues, or conclude if they can't be resolved, that it's best to leave the relationship properly—now, that's relief; emotional freedom. Though the grass may in fact look greener from where you're standing, myopically, you can't see the slippery slope a few feet away. Rest assured, it will come to greet you.

People also get caught up in chat rooms, sexting, online porn, and numerous websites that cater to the non-fidelity crowd. Technology brings a whole new component to the arena. You can actually create another persona for yourself and communicate anonymously in the most unseemly fashion from the comfort of your home. Settle in with a pbj sandwich, a bag of chips, and a nice glass of milk. Next thing you know, you are the sexiest thing going. You can live out your greatest fantasies from afar. It's not really cheating because you haven't touched anyone, right? Unless your significant other has the knowledge and is accepting, then, wrong. By the way, I'm not talking about a healthy, pleasurable fantasy life with spice thrown in for good measure. I'm talking about detrimental coveting. If you're hiding something from your mate that has the potential to cause undue emotional harm (and possible physical harm), get thee to Fidelity 101 in a quick hurry, it appears you've missed a chapter or two along the way. It's time to reassess your commitment and adjust accordingly.

Don't want to give up your routine and creature comforts that you've worked so hard to acquire? Then consider the shoe being on the other foot. Seriously consider it and take stock of your emotions. Take a few minutes to sit and *consciously* think about your significant other doing what you have done. Close your eyes and catch a glimpse of her/him sitting in front of the computer writing the exact same words you use to stimulate yourself and the object of your seduction—do this. This is your personal assignment. Every time you instigate communication with your cyber pal, think about the adrenalin rush and sexual stimuli your mate is *also* capable of feeling given the same circumstances. Think about the erotic photos that your mate is likewise able to ogle. How's that make you feel? What's going in your head? Are you uncomfortable or still rooted in denial? Incensed, affronted, deflated, sad—but still think you won't get caught? Too late. If you've participated in any of the extracurricular activity mentioned above, you're already caught up in your own snare of dishonesty.

There's also the Ashley Madison website that caters to those who are married or in a supposed committed relationship, yet want to have actual physical affairs. It has millions of members. That's an extraordinary amount of bank people are feeding into. When you engage in this type of service you are paying handsomely for someone *else's* opulent lifestyle. That's right; someone else is lazily yachting around the Riviera thanks to your generous donation. Awfully charitable of you. Chances are, once discovered, you can kiss that out-of-pocket diversion good-bye, along with most everything else you have of value, including your dignity. Ahhh…the nasty, cold grip of payback.

To reiterate from an earlier chapter, what is decided between people in regards to their relationship status and how they choose to conduct it, is between them. Whatever is discussed and agreed to as being acceptable, is (within the bounds of common law), until it's determined otherwise by the parties involved. Not just randomly and secretly by one and not the other. *Everyone* has to be on board. Of course there are numerous instances where one person doesn't want the relationship to end, in which case, you've still got to remove yourself from the relationship if it is wreaking havoc in your life or you just don't want it anymore. These are not easy circumstances, but they must be handled in a manner that doesn't encourage more ruin along the way, for your sake and all else involved.

What about sexting? No touchy-feely here so how can it be cheating? Well, if you're promoting yourself with seductive words and sending photos with provocative poses to another who is *not* your mate, you have some 'splaining to do. Again, consider if your mate was to do the same. Imagine your girlfriend/boyfriend/spouse texting enticing words and sending alluring pictures to some unknown individual. Would you appreciate them exposing themselves, literally and figuratively speaking, without your awareness? I didn't think so.

How about an untamed, intoxicating carnal episode with someone other than your at-this-point *in*significant other? You're at the local watering hole, get drunk, are frustrated as hell and don't give a crap. You're done, you're through, whatever....You scan the bar and spot the perfect person for your diversion. She's/he's ready, willing and able. You make a beeline into some room to have a playdate. You're both horny and raring to go. But wait, what about protection? Who's got protection? You weren't planning this, and who knows about the other? That's the point, you don't know about the other! STDs, HIV/AIDS, wacko, sado-masochist, rapist, stalker, someone just wanting to get pregnant? You *don't* know. Cheating is risky business on these merits alone. There is no point of reference, input from others, or a history to arm yourself with to make a smart choice. As if anything of this nature is a smart choice. Is it worth it? Is one selfish night of distraction worth the time and energy you've put into building something? Yes, your relationship foundation may be unstable, but now you've managed to land yourself in quicksand with no rope in sight, except for the figurative one to hang yourself. Well played.

What about being in the thick of an affair? It took some time, but you did manage to engage yourself in a bona fide affair, not a series of one-night stands. You're feeling pretty good about the fact that you're not sleeping around indiscriminately. You have a new boyfriend/girlfriend, *and* another half—three kids, two dogs, a bird, a trying job, unceasing bills, your Thursday night Meetup...aaand...the PTA meetings, dinner with friends and family, girls'/boys' night out, kids' sports, school recitals, doctor appointments, yadda, yadda, yadda.

Your paramour requests to see you at least two times a week. She/he is getting a bit more demanding. Time has gone by and emotions have been invested. Promises have been made in the heat of passion. Hopes are running high. Pressure mounts. Now *your* emotions are being pulled and stretched. Your world is slowly closing in. What to do? This is the part in the TV shows where a little dose of coolant slipped into Gatorade helps eliminate some of the cumbersome issues, or the unaware mate accidentally falls into the bathtub and drowns, or you find yourself the focus of in-your-face cameras with Joey Greco by your side and your screaming, fuming beloved on the other with a gazillion viewers glued to the tube waiting with bated breath for the pyrotechnics to ignite. Not ideal circumstances. Granted, some of these are extreme examples which no one wants to see happen, but they are by no means out of the realm of possibility.

Okay, so in spite of what common sense dictates, such as: lust only goes so far, the novelty of the situation will wear thin, and the shoulder to cry on will soon tire of the story, you've decided your lover is the one for you. She is all that your mate isn't. He is the answer to your every problem. You've managed to keep your affair under wraps. You've managed to placate your spouse and kids and obligations. However, you've decided to give the game away and exit stage left. You finally tell your mate you don't wish to be in the relationship any longer and are planning on moving out. Said mate is shocked, hurt, humiliated and asks that you give it another chance. Nope, you've made up your mind. You have nothing left to give. There's nothing more to be said. It's a done deal. Of course, you never in truth tried, but, oh, well. You do your best with the kids (mommy/daddy is going away for a while, but don't worry I'll come see you), or you leave it up to your mate to work it out. She's/he's better at that. You don't think the kids will miss you much anyway.

At last you can breathe and live a more satisfied life. Paramour is ecstatic, she/he won. The two of you have your very own love nest. This latest arrangement works well for a while. Of course paramour has to deal with the ex who is doling out grief in large amounts and the kids constantly cry (I guess they do miss you), but there's nothing that can't be overcome. Your bond is strong and true, except, what's this? A little tension in the new household. The divorce is starting to get sticky. Paramour doesn't seem so accepting these days. Looks like a few of the promises are going to have to be scaled back. Funds are flying out the door for alimony and child support. Paramour is not happy, not…one…bit…of happy. In fact, paramour is coincidentally starting to sound like the ex. Wow, that was quick. There's a whole lotta griping going on. Overtime at work is necessary to keep up with the old and new bills; more griping. Paramour is starting to care less and go out more. You're putting in maximum overtime to acquire minimum stress at the lost-love-nest. Not working. Paramour gets a hankering for milk from a dairy in parts unknown…

Your used-to-know is having none of you. The kids are angry. Your bank account is near ground zero. What you wouldn't give for a heart-to-heart with your ex, a good therapy session or ten, and a few hugs from your children. Exactly—you are where you are because of what you wouldn't give. *Now* you realize how much you care, but unfortunately…they…don't.

Chapter 7

Some Fun Facts and Enlightening Stats

This chapter is chockfull of figures and such. I thought it might be a good idea to share data that illustrates the impact that can occur when fidelity has been in question. Yes, the eyes tend to blur and the mind starts to wander, but statistics and visual aids are a sure way to get a quick shot of what's happening, or the potential thereof. Ignorance is nowhere near bliss in this respect. It will be worth your time and effort to at least *glance* in this direction.

For the record: speculation, variance in polling and the unknown are some components that affect statistics. The following stats are not absolutes, but are presented for informational purposes and your careful consideration. A variety of websites have been referenced. The Web info is presented is in its original form, with added personal commentary here and there.

(Findings provided by www.divorcerate2011.com)

Divorce Statistics in the United States

Almost 49 percent of the marriages end up in divorces.

Some Fun Facts and Enlightening Stats

- First marriages end up in divorces in an average duration of just less than 8 years
- 60 percent of all divorces are related to individuals aged 25 to 39
- There were more than 21 million divorces in the year 2000. In the same year, 58 million couples were married and still lived separated
- The average male age for a second divorce was 40.4 years and the average female age was 37.3 years in 1990
- The divorce rate of first time marriages is almost 10 percent less than the divorce rate for second marriages
- Over a 40 year period, 67 percent of first marriages terminate in a divorce and 50 percent of these divorces take place within the first 7 years
- Every year more than 1 million children are affected by divorce

Infidelity Divorce Statistics in America

In the United States 17 percent of the divorces have infidelity as their origin.

- A survey was conducted in the United States whether adultery should be considered as a crime –
    - 61 percent are of the opinion that it should not be
    - 35 percent thought it should be
    - 4 percent did not have any opinion
- Time-CNN conducted a poll regarding whether President Clinton's adultery has proved that his moral standard is identical to the average married man. 50 percent of the individuals in the United States replied 'yes' to the above statement.
- 90 percent of the persons in the United States are of the opinion that adultery is morally wrong.

- 14 percent of women and 22 percent of men acknowledged that they had sexual relations with an individual other than the married partner. These percentages in 1997 were 3 percent for women and 5 percent for men.
- 54 percent of married men and 70 percent of married women had no knowledge of the extramarital activities of their married partners.
- The infidelity statistics are high in case of young people. As a matter of fact, young men and young women are equally likely to be unfaithful.
- During the married life, 14 percent of married women and 22 percent of married men had extra-marital affairs minimum once.
- Infidelity has an inherent secrecy and hence it is difficult to determine the exact number of individuals who are having affairs.
- 65 percent of women and 75 percent of men acknowledge that they have sex with their co-workers.
- 81 percent of women and 86 percent of men acknowledge that they flirt with the opposite sex as a routine.
- 75 percent of men and 66 percent of women reveal that they have sexual thoughts about the people they work with.
- After an affair has been found out or accepted, 31 percent of marriages survive the discovery.
- The average duration of an affair is 2 years.
- 17 percent of men and women have acknowledged infidelity with a sister-in-law or brother-in-law, which might be of an emotional or physical type.
- In 41 percent of the marriages, one or both spouses accept they have committed infidelity, which may be physical or emotional.
- 38 percent of individuals have had explicit sexual conversation online.

Some Fun Facts and Enlightening Stats

- 50 percent of persons make a phone contact after they chat with somebody online.
- The Internet is used to flirt by 57 percent of the people.

For the question, "Should adultery be prosecuted in courts?" 67 percent replied 'Yes' and 33 percent replied 'No.' That's more than a fair amount of people who seem to be riled up about adultery. While I don't believe adultery is a crime, it certainly deserves its just due via a lawful penalty of sorts. A re-evaluation unquestionably *needs* to be done because something definitely ain't working, but more on that in Chapter 10, The Change-Up.

Now on to money. The Big Kahuna. You are gambling with your livelihood in the worst way when you decide to venture into an emotional hideaway. This is one estimated average household income before taxes: $63,091. Refer to the breakdown following the graph:

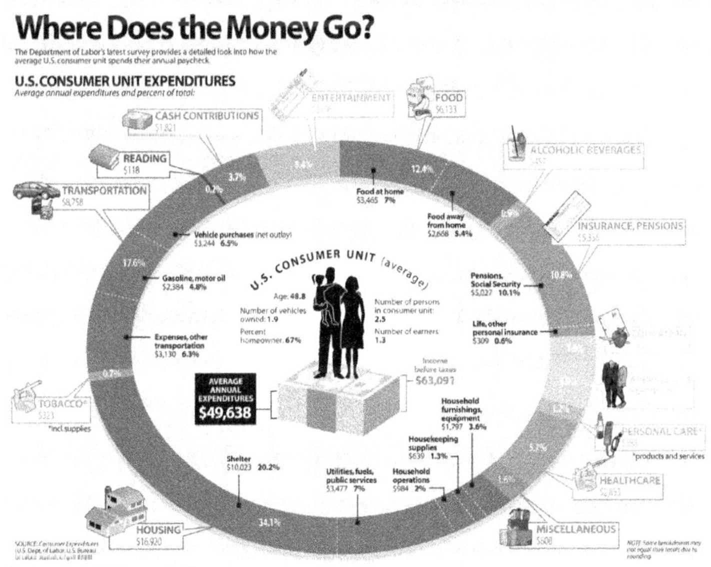

Source: Visual Economics

The average consumer has a budget that is split into a large number of monthly and yearly spending. The average consumer spends $49,638 a year on a range of necessary and desired expenditures. These expenditures come out of an annual household income of $63,091 per year on average, before taxes. The average consumer owns 1.9 vehicles, and 67 percent of them are homeowners. Households average 2.5 people and 1.3 earners reside in each. The largest expenditure of the average household is housing. This takes up an average 34.1 percent of the yearly budget of households. This is an average of $16,920 spent on housing. This amount includes $10,023 spent on shelter, $3,477 spent on public services and utilities, $984 spent on household operations, $639 spent on housekeeping supplies and 3.6 percent spent on household furnishings and equipment.

Are you still with me? Excellent. The second largest expenditure for the average consumer is transportation. The cost of vehicles purchased is an average of $3,244 per year, making it 6.5 percent of the average budget. The cost of oil and gas for vehicles costs the average consumer $2,384 per year, for an average of 4.8 percent of the total yearly budget. Combined, the cost of vehicles and their maintenance costs consumers an average of $8,758 per year. This is a total of 17.6 percent of the yearly budget.

Another large expenditure is healthcare, and as we all know, that may change for better or worse, depending. The average consumer spends $2,853 on healthcare each year. Another physical necessity, food, costs consumers an average of $6,133 per year. An average of $3,465 of that is spent on food that is consumed at home, and $2,668 of it is spent on food consumed away from home. Combined, the money spent on food is 12.4 percent of the entire yearly household budget. There is also, $323 a year on tobacco and $457 a year on alcoholic beverages. The average spending on clothing is $1,881.

To some the average income is chicken feed, to others wealth. Point being, when a marriage is rescinded potentially *half* of the finances and property go away (depending on where you live). Per this example: that's roughly $31,545, a substantial amount to see go by the wayside. That number is then decreased by the number of children in the household and their needs. And they will have plenty of needs. Some schools aren't able to provide essential supplies, which means that money has to come out of pocket from ma and pa. Extra-curricular activities will put another dent into the incredible shrinking wallet. What about you? Aren't you due a little diversion after all the stresses of the break-up? Nope. Golf and spa days are now past-tense. Feeling the pinch yet? How's a cramped apartment looking after having had your sprawling dream home? How 'bout that "new" used fifteen-year-old car that will probably need major maintenance at some point? Don't you wish you didn't spend that money on your paramour for that oh-so-romantic trip to wherever? Yep, para-no-more.

To add insult to injury, it's particularly devastating if there is only one working partner and the other is left to start over, sometimes penniless, and as a single parent. Here are some poverty threshold facts by way of www.ASPE.hhs.gov and www.census.gov for reflection. This report is based upon how many people are living in the household and the annual income within that household. When all is said and done, you may indeed find yourself hovering over the statistics below.

# of People in Household	Annual Income
1 (under 65 yrs. old)	$11, 702
2 (under 65 yrs. old)	$15, 504
3 (under 65 yrs. old)	$18,123
4 (under 65 yrs. old)	$22,891

It is also noted on www.dhcs.ca.gov re: 2011-2012 Federal Poverty Level Chart for Presumptive Eligibility, that an *unborn* child is also considered a person within the household.

Think about it: On some level, we make money to live, so that we can afford to die. Why sully life with *preventable* financial set-backs? When it comes to money, there are no limits as to what some may do if their livelihood has been threatened by an indiscretion. How many seething mates fight tooth and manicured nail to rip open the pocketbook and inflict deep revenge on the straying party? Take a guess. It's somewhere between mucho and mucho mas. Some are successful, others not. Either way, raging emotions alone do enough damage without the monetary snag. Medusas and Wendigos are having at it: deathmatch. No one wants to get caught in that chaos, but guess who does? The children. The innocents that you lovingly created. See how that plays out…

(More stats below via www.divorcerate2011.com)

Children of Divorce Statistics

- Assume that 'c' number of children are born to married parents during a year. Then, half of 'c' would witness the divorce of their parents before they complete 18 years of age.

Some Fun Facts and Enlightening Stats

- 40 percent of the children in the United States are growing up in the absence of their fathers.
- Consider that 'm' number of children have witnessed their parents divorce. Amongst these 'm' children, 1 out of 10 would further experience 3 or more parental marriage breakups.
- If there are 'n' number of children in the United States, then 50 percent of 'n' will go through the dissolution of their parent's marriage. Almost 25 percent of 'n' would experience the breakup of the parent's 2nd marriage.

Physical Harm – Children of Divorce Statistics

The possibility that a child would be beaten or murdered is 10 times more in a house where a female is the head as compared to a house that has both parents.

- Out of the total cases of child molestation, the majority are children of drug ring members or belong to single parent houses.
- As compared with children residing in broken homes, those children who live with their biological parents are 20 to 35 percent physically healthier.
- The possibility that children would develop health problems is 50 percent more after divorce as compared to families having both the parents.
- The possibility that children would experience speech defects, headaches, asthma, or injury is more after divorce when compared with children whose parents are married.

Emotional Pain – Children of Divorce Statistics

- Children of divorced parents develop more psychological problems even when compared with children from homes affected by cases of death.
- In a given year, teenagers in blended families and single parent families are *3 times more in need of psychological help.*
- During the 1980s, studies were executed and it was concluded that children who have experienced repeat divorces generally scored lesser grades. The peers of these children developed an opinion that it is less pleasant to be with them as compared to other children.

Long Term Effects of Divorce on Children

Out of the total long-term prison inmates, 70 percent are raised in broken homes.

- Six years after a parental marriage breakup, the children of such parents are generally insecure, anxious, unhappy, and lonely.

Other Crucial Statistics

Children are benefited by residing with parents who do not divorce. Their peers, who are children of divorced parents are approximately 2 times more likely to drop out of high school.

- ***The possibility of children attempting suicide is doubled*** regarding children who are related to broken homes when compared with children from non-broken houses.

Some Fun Facts and Enlightening Stats

- The children of divorced parents, and more specifically males, are usually more aggressive in behavior towards others.
- There is 4 times more possibility that children who have gone through their parent's divorce would report problems with friends and peers.
- In case of children belonging to fatherless homes:
    - 85 percent have behavioral disorders
    - 90 percent are homeless and runaway children
    - 63 percent commit youth suicide

You may think these statistics do not apply to you, however, no matter which financial strata you straddle, a less than favorable outcome is possible and quite probable. All this speaks for itself. Are you listening?

Now let's examine some other divorce info found at: www.livestrong.com, circa August 2011.

No-Fault Divorce

A "no-fault" divorce is any divorce in which the spouse asking for divorce does not have to prove that the other spouse did anything wrong. Often, it is enough simply to state that the parties cannot successfully get along anymore. Most U.S. states offer no-fault divorce, but a few require a period of separation before a no-fault divorce will be granted.

States with No-Fault Divorce and No Waiting Period

The states that offer no-fault divorce *without* requiring a period of separation are:

Alaska, Arizona, California, Colorado, Florida, Georgia, Indiana, Iowa, Kansas, Kentucky, Maine, Massachusetts, Michigan, Mississippi, Missouri, Montana, Nebraska, New Hampshire, New Mexico, North Dakota, Oklahoma, Oregon, South Dakota, Washington, Wisconsin, and Wyoming.

In these states, a couple may obtain a no-fault divorce without first meeting any separation requirement. Some of these states also offer legal separation instead of divorce.

No-Fault Divorce with Separation Requirements

Some states require the parties to live apart for a minimum length of time before seeking a no-fault divorce. The length of time required varies by state and ranges from 180 days to five years. The states that require a period of separation, and the minimum length of separation, are:

Alabama - 2 years
Connecticut - 18 months
Hawaii - 2 years
Idaho - 5 years
Illinois - 2 years
Louisiana - 180 days
Minnesota - 180 days
Nevada - 1 year
Ohio - 1 year
Pennsylvania - 2 years
Rhode Island - 3 years
Tennessee - 2 years
Texas - 3 years
Utah - 3 years
West Virginia - 1 year

No-Fault and Fault Divorce States

Some U.S. states offer both a no-fault and at-fault divorce option. Couples who do not want to observe the waiting period requirement are allowed to file for fault divorce. Some common grounds for fault include cruelty, adultery, desertion, confinement in prison or a similar institution, and inability to perform sexual intercourse, if this was not disclosed prior to the marriage. States that offer both no-fault and fault divorce include:

Alabama, Alaska, Connecticut, Delaware, Georgia, Idaho, Illinois, Maine, Massachusetts, Mississippi, New Hampshire, New Mexico, North Dakota, Ohio, Oklahoma, Pennsylvania, Rhode Island, South Dakota, Tennessee, Texas, Utah, and West Virginia

The next paragraph was written by, Cathy W. Meyer (www.cathywmeyer.com)

Equitable Distribution of Marital Property

There are two legal theories that govern how marital property is divided: Community Property or Equitable distribution. Equitable distribution is more common than community property laws and instead of requiring a 50/50 split of marital property; it takes into account the economic situation of each spouse. While equitable distribution is more flexible, it is also harder to forecast the outcome, since there are so many factors taken into consideration during settlement negotiations.

The following was news to me. I had never heard of it before, and I think that can be said for the majority of people. This item is from: www.legal-dictionary.thefreedictionary.com/Covenant+Marriage.

Covenant Marriage

The declining stability of U.S. marriages has been dramatic. In 2002, the CENSUS BUREAU issued a study that concluded almost half of all first marriages will end in divorce. The rise in the divorce rate began in the 1960s and accelerated in the 1970s, after most states enacted no-fault divorce laws, which made it much easier for married couples to dissolve their marriage contracts. By the 1990s, a small but vocal number of people argued that it was too easy to divorce. Prior generations of husbands and wives had worked out their problems and preserved their marriages. Current divorce laws allowed couples to quit a marriage at the first sign of trouble.

These concerns led Louisiana, in 1997, to enact the first covenant marriage law in the United States (L.S.A.-R.S. 9:272 et seq. [1997]). The law created two forms of marriage in the state: the traditional *marriage contract*, with minimal formalities of formation and dissolution, and a *covenant marriage*, which imposes heightened requirements for entering and leaving a marriage. Supporters of the covenant marriage law saw it as a way to strengthen marriages and families. They were troubled over the creation of a marriage contract that had religious connotations—the word *covenant* is associated in Christianity with a contract between man and God. Opponents expressed doubts. Critics also pointed out that there would be additional costs associated with the additional requirements.

The law mandates three significant requirements for couples who choose to enter into a covenant marriage: (1) the couple must legally agree to seek marital counseling if problems develop during the marriage; and (2) the couple can only seek a divorce or legal separation for limited reasons. In addition, before obtaining a covenant marriage license, the couple must receive premarital counseling from a priest, minister, rabbi, clergyman of any religious sect, or a professional marriage counselor.

Once married, a husband and wife are expected to commit to a lifetime partnership. However, the law recognizes that some couples will want to separate or divorce. The covenant marriage provisions require a spouse to first obtain counseling and then prove one or more grounds for separation or divorce as listed in the statute. This is the key difference between the two types of marriage: in essence, a spouse has to prove fault by the other spouse. The grounds for legal separation are: Adultery by the other spouse; commission of a felony by the other spouse and a sentence of imprisonment at hard labor, or death; abandonment by the other spouse for one year; physical or sexual abuse of the spouse or of a child of either spouse; the spouses have lived separate and apart for two years; or habitual intemperance (for example, alcohol or drug abuse), cruel treatment, or severe ill treatment by the other spouse. The reasons for divorce exclude this last ground but include the other four.

The enactment of the Louisiana law did not signal a swift change in marriage law preferences. In the first year only one percent of couples elected covenant marriage; the rate remains less than five percent. Advocates of covenant marriage introduced similar legislation in other states but the results have not been overwhelming. Arizona passed a covenant marriage law in 1998 (A.R.S. § 25-901 et seq. [1998]), but it is less restrictive in setting grounds for divorce and does not have a two-year waiting period. Arkansas passed its covenant marriage law in 2001 (Covenant Marriage Act of 2001, § 9-11-801 et seq.). At least 16 other state legislatures considered laws between 1999 and 2002, but failed to enact them.

It will take many years for researchers to assess the effectiveness of this type of marriage contract and to determine whether it helps couples avoid divorce. The small number of couples who seek covenant marriage may be the very ones who would have succeeded with a traditional marriage, as they have demonstrated a serious commitment to making their marriages last.

Here is some eye-opening data per our good friends at Wikipedia (search "Adultery" entry for the annotated reference guide):

In the traditional English common law, adultery was a felony. Although the legal definition of "adultery" differs in nearly every legal system, the common theme is sexual relations outside of marriage, in one form or another.

For example, New York defines an adulterer as a person who "engages in sexual intercourse with another person at a time when he has a living spouse, or the other person has a living spouse." North Carolina defines adultery as occurring when any man and woman "lewdly and lasciviously associate, bed, and cohabit together." Minnesota law provides: "when a married woman has sexual intercourse with a man other than her husband, whether married or not, both are guilty of adultery." As recently as 2001, Virginia prosecuted an attorney, John R. Bushey of Luray, for adultery, a case that ended in a guilty plea and a $125 fine. Adultery is *against* the governing law of the U.S. military.

In the United States, laws vary from state to state. In those states where adultery is still on the statute books (although rarely prosecuted), penalties vary from life sentence (Michigan) to a $10 fine (Maryland) to a Class B misdemeanor (New York) to a Class I felony (Wisconsin).

In the U.S. Military, adultery is a potential court-martial offense. The enforceability of adultery laws in the United States is unclear following Supreme Court decisions since 1965 relating to privacy and sexual intimacy of consenting adults. However, occasional prosecutions do occur.

Who knew? Legal and religious interpretations of adultery vary widely amid world cultures, from nonchalance and acceptance, to ostracization and stoning. The better deal is probably not to err on the side of almost certain backlash.

If the United States is witnessing an uprising, take note of this article, "Adultery on the Increase," in The Zimbabwean (www.thezimbabwean.co.uk), by Tawanda Majoni (the byline states John Makumbe as the author, which was in error, Mr. Majoni in fact penned this). I have condensed his article for the sake of space, but the gist is clear. Please do research and read it in its entirety. It's highly edifying.

"I have elected this week to explore the social arena, where a fatal malignance - infidelity within marriage - seems to be spreading by the day…Men are the major culprits, as they have always been. But I have observed that women are fast catching up…The burning question is: Why does life in Zimbabwe now seem to revolve around this kind of sexual pleasure that should be spat at in a normal society? The answers below are based on my own observations and discussions with involved parties and colleagues. Increasing financial freedom gives women a sense of independence to do what she likes, or needs. More and more women can now fend for themselves and no longer have to rely on the chauvinist husband for their welfare. This has tended to boost their sense of choice. Nothing wrong with that if choice is deployed to socially acceptable activities, of course...Men do not make the situation any better. They are still steeped in that chauvinistic cauldron that women are fighting hard to escape from and think that the best way to bring women back into line is through mental, sexual, physical and emotional abuse. But this abuse drives women straight into the arms of other men as they seek solace and sympathy...Marital infidelity destroys marriages. It is certainly a driver of HIV/AIDS and who needs more orphans when the country has more than 1 million already? It undermines confidence in the social structure and produces a legion of miscreants."

As you can see by and large, the break-up of a couple and family due to fidelity gone astray lends itself to many distressing factors and daunting statistics. When divorce is involved the legal fees alone, even if it's done DIY (forms from the courthouse), a la We The People, or mediation, still cost money and should put things into perspective. Economically it can plunge people into murky areas of which they are not familiar or comfortable. This isn't just about an inconvenience or a hiccup with regards to your financial health. It can set the tone for bankruptcy and government aid. Society at large will then bear the fiscal downside. And, guess what? *You, too*, are "society at large"!

Not to mention, one's mental state can be greatly affected: depression, ongoing anger, acting out, possible suicide—the short list. Fortunately there are widespread resources for these challenges. But wouldn't it be wiser to address the problems in advance and help forestall negative impacts by way of your own progressive conscience? Ideally, it's a given.

Perhaps most disheartening is that children carry the burden of these adult issues. They are not equipped to comprehend these upheavals. They may find fault with themselves, as if it's something they've done to fracture the family. The weight of self-inflicted guilt, dread of abandonment, and dampened spirits, all contribute to who they may grow up to be.

It's glaringly evident the domestic socio-economic framework is at stake. I, for one, want to be on the side of prevention and rebuilding. Come join me.

Chapter 8

Bits of My Backstory

I guess it's only fair to include a few of my personal episodes for the credibility factor, or so "they" say. Those dang "they" people never let up. However, putting private matters into a public forum is no simple feat: a showdown between action and emotion. It's much easier to reflect upon, run it through your head, or verbalize to a few close allies. Once it's in print, it's bona fide (at least in this instance) and uncomfortable at best.

First, I'll start off with a little ditty that happened to me when I was in my late 20's, copious moons ago. It's an example of another version of impropriety. I was living in Beverly Hills and frequented the local post office. A very well-dressed gentleman was getting into his very well-dressed car and stopped to initiate conversation with me. He seemed non-threatening and asked a few questions about what I did (I was pursuing acting at the time), where I lived, etc. He was courteous and exceptionally nice. I was impressed by the fact he looked me directly in the eye while talking. He was possibly 40ish. His name was Giovanni, or Paolo, or something equally Italian sexy. He mentioned he had a clothing store and could use some help. Being that I needed to work other jobs until my big acting break decided to grace me with its presence, my curiosity was piqued. He quoted a nice salary, so I gave him my service number, not my home number. We said our good-byes and parted ways.

He phoned a couple of days later, we chatted further. After a few other subsequent conversations I agreed to meet with him to talk specifics about the job. We set a location and time. I met him at the appointed meeting place (a public restaurant/bar) and we exchanged pleasantries. I noticed he was holding a stack of greeting cards in envelopes—unsealed. He handed me one of the cards. I opened it. It held a sweet greeting, that I can't remember, but I do recall it was flattering. However, the card wasn't signed. He handed me a few others, same thing, sweet but not signed; personal, yet not. I'm sure he had a million of them for various occasions. Well, lo and quite a lot to behold, the last card I opened had five thousand big ones in it. 5k in greenbacks! He told me there was more where that came from. I held my composure (how, I'll never know) and waited for him to explain, although I pretty much knew what he was proposing.

Story was: he lived in Italy, although I detected an East Coast accent, with his wife. He traveled to L.A. for his clothing business and stayed with his aunt in Bel Air while in town. True, not true, who knows. The man was impeccably dressed and had a beautiful car, but again, who knows. He implied that he would be interested in "keeping me". He did not say those exact words, but the insinuation was apparent. I managed to keep a straight face. I told him I was due to move to Manhattan Beach, which was already in process. He didn't think that would be an inconvenience. Very accommodating of him. He said he would only be in town one week out of the month. Hm...well...he *was* exceedingly charming, maybe physically not my type, but he seemed normal enough. At least he didn't reek of smarmy. And who couldn't use 5k and then some, especially a struggling actress? I wasn't really struggling, but you get the idea. But, no. I politely told him I was flattered (in retrospect—really?), but it wasn't something I was interested in doing. I mentioned that there were plenty of other women who would gladly take him up on his offer. This is L.A. after all (sad, but true). He graciously accepted my reply. I wished him well, shook his hand and excused myself. I went into the elevator and then proceeded to laugh my ass off—all the way to my car. For some reason, I thought it was the funniest thing ever. I was taken aback in one sense, but on the flipside, I saw comedy in the ridiculousness of it.

I have to admit after the dust settled I gave it a brief passing thought. Yet how the heck was I going to explain a fancy condo, furniture, clothes, and a new car (I was in deeply imagined castle-in-the-sky-money-roll mode) to my parents? I loved them, and they me. They admired and respected me, for the most part, and I couldn't bear the thought of hurting them in that way. I certainly wasn't thinking about Giovanni/Paolo/Nunzio's wife, but at least I was thinking. So, I let it go. To this day the mere thought of it makes me laugh way-out-loud and I still don't know why.

On to a more prickly subject: my role as the "other" woman. I was never the other woman in the meet-you-same-time-same-place kind of affair. It was random over the course of time. There wasn't any talk of leaving the marriage for me, nor did I ask for or expect that. It was more about his marriage disintegrating, and I was the outlet of sorts. Wow—the outlet. Not a good way to see yourself metaphorically or otherwise. Take note, other women. However, conversely, our liaison was never fully consummated, per his request.

Apparently he didn't want to overstep the ultimate boundary that he set for himself. A perfect illustration of how we are inclined to rationalize our actions by our own perceived ethical standards. Interesting, that. Needless to say, he wasn't totally on board.

While in its own unique way there was genuine caring and concern between us, there were no professions of love and no future promises. Somehow that didn't bother me so much. It was more the excitement and anticipation of our next meeting. I wanted to be within his trajectory. I admired him for his background and his life accomplishments. I was invigorated by our conversations. I fed off that. The physical existed, but it wasn't the nucleus. I suppose that's an odd statement to make since sex seems to be the fuel for these smoldering fires. I sometimes did envision an authentic relationship, although it was never discussed, yet the responsibility of that wasn't so appealing. Strangely enough, it was somewhat frightening to think of taking it to the next level. Another uncommon thought for a woman in that situation, but I was pretty fine with the way things were. I dated other men and went about my business. Of course, maybe I didn't want to "want" it for fear it would never happen; a valid consideration that I have since recognized.

His marriage was in trouble without my participation and that made it more acceptable for me to be involved in such a way. I did not consider his wife. I did not consider damaging another woman in the process, or another human being for that matter. I never knew if she found out about me, but that shouldn't have had any bearing on my actions. Although I wasn't the actual philanderer, I was a more than willing participant. I was peripherally instrumental in helping to unravel the fabric of that marriage and spiritually compromising myself and others in the process. Not cool. Of course, I didn't think about this then. The non-thinking part seems to be a running theme for those who have had a fling with infidelity.

As life would have it, I became engaged. I never saw my partner in crime during my relationship, but I did call and tell him. Ironically enough, he was newly, officially separated. What?! How could the timing be so off? I loved my fiancé, but all that went before with the other man, with no real closure, sent my head spinning. He wished me well and said my fiancé was a lucky man. Nice sentiment, empty words. From my gut reaction I realized I had invested much more emotion than I had led myself to believe. Thankfully I was able to place my feelings out of harm's way and proceed with my impending marriage. Little did I know the shoe would be migrating to the other foot.

I looked forward to my marriage. I was 43 years old and felt I was *finally* ready. Although it did somewhat scare me, marriage was never a must-do in my world. For some of us it takes a little longer, if at all. I had a lengthy, satisfying singledom and felt prepared to tie the nuptial knot. There were red flags along the way, but I honestly thought they could be worked through. I had a solid view of what marriage should be and I was bound and determined to realize that perception.

I'm pleased to say I had a fantastic wedding. I continue to carry warm memories of that exceptional day. I couldn't have asked for anything more, except maybe to be wed in Spain, however, both our mothers were experiencing health issues, so we did the next best thing. We were married at a lovely sprawling estate with strong Spanish influences and décor.

Bits of My Backstory

I'm a Mexican-American from Southern California and my ex-husband is a Puerto Rican from Lower Eastside New York; because of our shared Spanish heritage our venue was an ideal cultural compromise. We had flamenco dancers, salsa music, Mexican music, American standards, basic and not so basic rock, and everything else in between. Our first dance was to Harry Connick, Jr.'s, "It Had To Be You." There's a line in the song that always reverberates with me: "…with all your faults I love you still." Spot on. I'm sure my groom felt the same way.

Then, the marriage began. As I mentioned, I had a precise vision of what a marriage should be. "Should" is indicative of some of the flaws in my theory at the time. I now know differently. To quote the wise Dona Margarita character from Victor E. Villasenor's book, *Rain of Gold*, "Marriage has only the value that a man and woman put on it." Simple, elegant, powerful words.

Like most marriages, ours had a honeymoon phase. We reveled in the newness of it and eventually found our rhythm. Unfortunately that rhythm became staccato. Although my ex and I were in the same industry (we met at work) and had similar interests and friends, we had distinct personalities. He's bright, creative, and sensitive. I share some of his traits, but I'm also more practical and have a thicker skin. A good balance for some, sadly not for us.

My ex had issues and needs that were indoctrinated at a very early age—a father matter. (I hear so much about fathers and how they adversely affect their son's lives. It's incredibly upsetting. This is a topic that requires much more attention.) I suppose I had my own issues in other areas, but I believed I had dealt with mine in a more productive manner. My ex had been married once before. He liked being married. I didn't have the experience, but I had an idealized version lodged in my cranium. I wanted to stick to my plan, not taking into account there was another real, live human being who wasn't programmed to do my bidding. Nevertheless, I was adamant about my image of marriage. He, in turn, carried his own arsenal of wants. Together we created plenty of conflict. We went to therapy, individually and as a couple. For therapy to be reasonably effective, both parties have to be consistent and in accordance with the learning curve. That's tricky for couples to comprehend and follow through. They want speedy fixes. It doesn't work that way. As for us, it was problematic to find our footing. Nonetheless, I was finally catching on. I was starting to understand the error of my ways and I was excited to make the changes. I foresaw a brighter future for us; a future that would never be brought to fruition.

Time passed but our battle wounds never completely healed. The emotional damage had permeated many other aspects of our marriage. During this period my ex was traveling frequently for a project. Due to our sporadic schedule together I wasn't able to wholly implement my transformation. I remained home when he traveled, and was fine with that. I did join him on occasion, but I didn't feel the need to follow him. I was independent in my own right and made good use of my personal time. Moreover, my ex was on a mission working toward his goal and went out often to make social contacts.

Before we get into the obvious writing on the wall, I'd like to share a distinctive addition to this story. I had called a psychic to inquire if my husband's upcoming project would be a success. FYI—I don't live and die by psychics, but I am one who freely gathers information from whatever sources I feel could be of value. She wasn't your typical 1-800 variety, of which I have no experience, this person was referred to me. I was on the phone with her less than two minutes when she told me, "There's been an infidelity in your marriage." I had said nothing to her. Nada. It wasn't even remotely on my radar. I laughed and told her, "Well, it isn't me!" I didn't bother to question her further. It was a non-issue. I continued on with the conversation about other matters. I didn't say a word to my husband about her statement. I told only one person, our therapist, just to have it on record, then, I left it alone. I did make a mental note, but I wasn't going to act on anything—because there wasn't anything to act on.

Back to the writing on the wall…As you may have already guessed, my ex wound up having an affair by way of one of his social outings. A couple of months after I had the session with the psychic, he told me he didn't think he wanted to be married anymore. At this time I still didn't know of the affair, but I did ask if he was having one. He replied in the negative, no. I assumed he was having difficulty dealing with our problems and needed time to think. So, I opted to move out. Sometimes you need to step away in order to come back together. I still had hopes we could make it work. Then another unusual thing happened. A month or so later I bolted out of the twilight state between sleeping and rising and utterly knew, without a single, solitary doubt, that he was undeniably having an affair. I grabbed my phone, called him, got his voice mail and went on a rant. I was livid and my language was vivid. It was stream of consciousness profanity, exceptionally lively and descriptive. I was beside myself with anger and disbelief. Yes, I had been forewarned, but it wasn't tangible evidence in my estimation. It didn't come from my own "knowing." However, at that moment in time I did, unquestionably, know.

My ex eventually returned my call. We fought and then he spilled the beans. Honestly, I was more angered and offended by the fact that he had lied to me about *not* having an affair, than the actual affair itself. He *lied* to me! By this point in life the essence of whom I was had been well-formed. My self-esteem never suffered from his conduct. Even though I was culpable on some level—I still knew who I was. At the onset of my marriage, I realized I was not immune to infidelity, but as is so typical with any striking disturbance, the impact is unknown until it hits *you*. In hindsight, there were only three signs of something amiss. The first one: we were still under the same roof. The phone rang, I answered and whomever it was hung up. I jokingly told my husband, "Your girlfriend called." He didn't comment. Yeah, ha-ha. The second one: we were in the car and it smelled heavily of (yes, I'm going to say it) cheap perfume. I commented on it. He said his sister had been with him the day before. I was around his sister fairly often and knew this wasn't an aroma she'd choose. The third one: after I had moved out I suggested we have date nights to help work through our troubles. He said it was too much pressure. Seriously?! Hey, I'm your wife! Yes, it hurt, but I thought he needed more time to mull things over—and mull he did. It wasn't long after the affair was revealed that he told me this woman was pregnant. Remember I said he had a father matter that affected him? His father had left his mother for another woman and had a child out of wedlock: the apple and the tree.

My life was arduous thereafter. Pain, fury, astonishment, and all the other oft-told illustrative words used in similar circumstances were my companions. I didn't let him off the hook, nor did I try and stop him from what he was doing. The updated development in his affair didn't lend much to that end. When his child was born our divorce was still pending, but in process. Technically we were still married, which in essence made me his child's stepmother. How's that for crazy? I went through an extremely trying time. All kinds of crap hit the fan; finances, emotions, etc. I shifted into auto-pilot to keep my head on straight. I'm a pretty tough cookie, but this was an immense challenge on many levels. Had the finances not been an issue, I would have fared much better. Unfortunately, that wasn't my reality.

Regrettably, I was never given the chance to show my true potential as a mate. I felt that was unfairly taken from me. I wanted to make things right, but he had already turned the corner. Yet there was an upside to all this, as strange as that may sound. I chose to live near my immediate family during this ordeal and was fortunate enough to spend quality time with my mother before her death. Having lost my sweet, funny father many years prior, I understood the importance of time well spent with this amazing woman. As a matter of fact, because of this chaotic upheaval, my mother was just about the only person I wanted to spend any time with. In some senses we became "mother and child" again. I really needed her. I almost have to thank my ex for that—almost.

Due to the nature of this book, it's not entirely fair to solely present my side of this story, so I phoned my ex and asked him a few questions. It's been about six years since the incident and I wanted to get his take on things at this stage. Whether I agree with his reasoning or not won't be debated. This is his truth, not mine.

Ex's version (Reader's Digest condensed)

Because I was somewhat hesitant to get married, he felt I was settling for him. He wishes he would have listened to his instincts to override some of my decisions. He thought I was pushy and controlling. His needs weren't being met. He didn't feel like he was being cared for. We were more like roommates. He felt we were going in different directions planning-wise. He didn't think there was a future for us. He wanted to escape, but he didn't know how to tell me. He needed a breath of fresh air.

He met someone (she knew he was married) that paid attention to him. She satisfied his needs. Yet the relationship with her became worse than ours. Had she not been pregnant he would have considered working on us because he saw my willingness to do so. He admits to wrong-doing. He's very remorseful and sorry it happened. He feels guilty how he went about things. His life has been difficult ever since. The only good thing that came from the affair is his daughter.

Yes, he did the cheating, but I readily admit I was also accountable. He was responsible for committing the act, I was responsible for contributing to it. I have since implemented new-found skills; with a few ounces of thought and foresight I hope not to repeat the same mistakes. It takes two to make or break a relationship. It's rare that only one party is the "victim." Victim is an overused word for these situations. My ex was the perpetrator, but I also brought injurious issues to the table. We've apologized to each other and have managed to maintain a friendship throughout the years, albeit with a few stops and starts, but we continue to move forward. We care about each other in a way that will keep us connected for years on end. In spite of the history, he remains a very special person in my life. Besides, we still have some unfinished business that I fully expect to be remedied.

As a startling side note: my lovely hand-made, off the shoulder, silk charmeuse and Chantilly-lace (with a sultry line of buttons down the back) wedding gown was destroyed in a fire at the drycleaners where it was being *preserved*. Irony in fine form. To add insult to injury, the insurance company that was assisting the cleaners with the claims stated the gown had depreciated, although it had only been a few months post-wedding. *No* dress, for even less…No one sees this coming.

Personally, I try to live by the "do unto others…" principle. Being a mere mortal, it takes daily perseverance. But, with the sketchy subject matter of infidelity, I find it to be a no-brainer. Aside from the instantaneous psychological and spiritual damage it does to all parties involved, it takes waaay too much energy. Who can keep track of all the lies?! Too much work. Not to mention, that *willingly* adding stress upon stress is clearly nonsensical. Now if JFK, Jr. was still amongst us it would be tempting for sure. However, he's resting peacefully and I will never be taken to task.

Postscript: my ex's relationship with the other woman didn't last. Like I didn't know that was going to happen. Newsflash—rebounds rarely do; another reason to stay the reputable course. As I mentioned, my ex is thankful for his daughter. He loves her madly, as well he should. I've met her. She's a very sweet, bright child. I wonder if they'll ever tell her about the circumstances of which she was conceived. And the session I had with the psychic? Turns out the affair was instigated the same month as my reading.

Post postscript: Now I know what it feels like…for what it's worth, my deepest apologies.

Chapter 9

The Change-Up

If you've read thus far, chances are you would like to consciously reflect on fidelity as a better option. You're determined to shift your thinking and advance your life. Kudos to you! It takes an incredible amount of courage to examine your flaws and want to right them, or at least attempt to make them more workable. It takes equal amounts of courage to recognize that whom you choose as a mate will more than likely have hurdles that, without a doubt, will require *your* sensitivity and understanding. This is unquestionably a two-way street. Perfection in human form does not exist. We all carry variable amounts of baggage and damage that help shape who we are. It is our individual duty to be accountable for our actions, *despite* the actions of others. Very important, that. Here are some digestible tidbits to help you along in everyday life.

Primarily, you have to be cognizant of how you may be causing unwarranted harm to yourself, your mate, and the relationship. If you're not going to tend to yourself with a candid approach, prepare to keep spinning on the cycle you're riding—to absolutely nowhere except around that wonky little road you keep circling. A significant amount of energy is expended with useless repetition. This energy could be applied toward implementing a superior way of being, a far better use of time.

It's imperative to put yourself on the line. There's no way around it. *You* are your own threshold. If you can't see the forest for the trees, ask around. Ask trusted friends and family to give you feedback on behavior they have noticed that may be preventing you from having more balanced relationships. If you value their opinion, you will undoubtedly uncover some unknowns, or find substantiation for what you've already suspected yet haven't dared tackle. Listen with an open mind. Try not to judge or become defensive—just listen. Take from it what you can. You may or may not be completely ready to deal with yourself, but taking *any* sort of first step is a mighty fine one. Give yourself time to assimilate the information. How are you responding internally? If it's an emotional knee-jerk reaction, step back and sit with it a while longer. If you're receiving the same comments over and over again from reliable sources, pay close attention. It will behoove you to examine how that explicit behavior has played out in your romantic associations. Attempt to look at it from a purely observational point of view. Imagine if someone else exhibited that same behavior and how *you* would respond to it. Your aha! moment.

If you're not ready to face yourself head-on, there are support groups for practically any type of situation. Find your fit by getting references from others, researching on the Internet, or letting your fingers do the walking in the Yellow Pages. Whatever it takes, do it. Support groups exist for a similar goal: finding the best possible way to deal with running themes that aren't serving a constructive purpose. Sharing in a group environment with like-minded people will help alleviate your fears. If you're hearing your story come out of someone else's mouth, you *know* you're not alone. A safe environment will nurture your growth and allow you the space to feel comfortable while discussing your distinct circumstances.

If you don't know where to start, but definitely know there is a problem at hand, consult with whomever you find reassurance. Consider counseling/therapy (which come in a range of styles), confer with a spiritual advisor, or your friendly neighborhood guru. There's no reason to feel this isn't for you. That's what it's there for—you. Inquire with your health insurance carrier, some cover mental health counseling. Don't let the words mental health conjure up any negative notions. There is *no* stigma in having the courage to develop and grow! If deficient monies cause you to hesitate, many therapists offer a sliding scale. Voice your financial position, more than likely you will find someone who will kindly work within your limits. There are also counselors that offer free first sessions, either in the office or over the phone. Use this to your advantage. Again, *your* due diligence is required with regards to making inquiries that will guide you along. Be advised that in a one-on-one therapy situation it's essential you find someone with whom you are relaxed and compatible. If not, you may find yourself considerably more stressed and will have sufficiently defeated your purpose. It's necessary to establish an ongoing rapport with your therapist. As in all relationships, to receive an optimal outcome you have to be consistent. It's difficult to achieve measurable results if you are not allowing progress to take its course. Unfortunately, most people head into therapy when they're in intense crisis mode. They are eager for answers and fixes in the moment. Not gonna happen. Therapy is rarely a one-time occurrence. Understand that your improved behavior will not transpire in one session. If it's taken decades to create the distressing matter, it's by no means going away overnight. It takes time, patience, and doing the work. Yes, there is work involved, like anything else that yields encouraging results when effort is put forth. This is where you have to fully commit to *yourself*. You have to value your own identity and work from there. There is good selfish and bad selfish. This is good selfish. It's okay. You're worth every bit, don't let anyone else influence your decision. Promote your life. Allow yourself the privilege of having your new way of being enfold before you.

Examples of behaviors and issues that can stymie one's growth are: fear, stress, denial, pride, anger, trauma, aggression, boredom, insecurity, passivity, loss of libido, co-dependence, addiction, violence, excessive compliance, depression, unrealistic expectations, and lack of emotional support, to name quite a few. If you identify with any of the aforementioned and verifiable discomfort in your relationship is a consequence, seek help. Regarding anger and acting out; these actions are usually indicative of a core hurt that has never been identified or is purposefully being suppressed. You may feel justified by masking the pain with overt forms of "protection" instead of dealing with it head on, but it's counterproductive nonetheless. All that explosive expended energy eventually takes its toll. When these topics border on unstable and suitable tools and skills are not implemented, fidelity can recede into the background. Remember, ultimately, *you* are in control your life, not external situations or someone else's problems. You may feel trapped, guilty, irate, wronged, and a litany of other responses, but it still boils down to how *you* react to your environment.

What about triggers? Triggers are those pesky stimuli in the form of words, expressions or events that set you off. You go from 0 to 1,000 in a hot instant. No sooner does your mate make that particular "face" and you're in the def-con zone. You're on high alert and ready to release the hounds. This is a tough one, but believe it or not, something as simple as counting to ten comes in very handy. If you can only make it to five, or two, at least you give yourself some respite from reaction. Test yourself by expanding your length of counting each time. Keep going back to it until the overwhelming rush of your reaction starts to fade. This will take some time, but trust yourself to see it through. On the other hand, if it's something your mate can pull back on, have a discussion about the possibility of reducing or eliminating that bothersome instance. Ask your mate to be patient while you try and adjust your behavior. Relationships are a collaboration. Keep in mind, your mate is bound to have triggers where you're concerned as well. Be amenable and open to suggestions coming your way.

Then there's communication, communication, communication; the granddaddy. I used to pride myself on being a great communicator; problem was, I was communicating *at* someone, not *with* them. Huge difference. Check yourself on this. Just because you're the one doing most of the talking, doesn't mean you're the one who is most effective. You may think you have all the answers, but truth is, you can learn from your mate—if you care to. You have to want to listen and be present. If your mate and relationship have meaning, be willing to acknowledge their specific needs, which may not automatically sync up to yours, but show respect by hearing them out. You don't necessarily have to agree, but understanding they have valid points will further your communication. By the way, the old maxim of agree to disagree is not a cop-out. It is a helpful way of allowing for opinions without malice or resentments.

Validation: another biggie. Everyone wants to have input. Everyone wants to feel heard. Everyone wants to be appreciated. We all want to be recognized on some level. That doesn't mean you have to kowtow, falsely acquiesce, or lie, it simply means give your mate credit for contributing to the union. Engage with him/her. Not the put-a-ring-on-it engaged, but rather the listening, conversing, involving yourself with them kind of engagement. If you tune out continually, it's guaranteed you're not going to receive goodwill in return. If you need your downtime, ask for it. It's fine to do so if it's not needlessly impeding the flow of your partnership. We all need our alone time. It's *healthy* to recharge your batteries. It doesn't mean the love is lost, it's not cause for paranoia and suspicion, it means you need to catch your breath. For some it's twenty minutes, for others its two days. Each relationship has its particular criteria.

We all want to be cared *about*, not necessarily taken care *of*, as in the strict financial sense. If there are two employed people in a relationship who do not require the finances of the other to live their life, then being cared about constitutes a large part of their union. If one works and the other stays at home, they take care of each other in a way that meets their defined needs. Those who don't want to be productive in their own right, whether that's working outside or inside the home, and solely want a free ride without contributing substantially to the relationship, will be largely disappointed. This is a quick way to find yourself in the line of fidelity under-fire. Foremost: you are not allowing yourself to develop your innate abilities, no matter what your previous circumstances. This is not meant to downplay traumas that may have fed into your character. If anything, it's meant to speak to your *fortitude*. Laziness, insecurities, and fear are not ample reasons to glom onto a meal ticket indefinitely.

Create your own ride. It's beneficial to be independent and take care of *your* business; as a matter of fact it should be obligatory at some point. It's your gain to develop your own skill set. Your mate won't be around forever. Life education is one of the most powerful resources to glean from. While formal education is obviously a boon in any situation, if you don't have the inclination or funds, check out an appropriate book at the library, attend classes, seminars, workshops, etc. that provide guidance and assistance on infinite subjects in short, efficient doses. Whatever your current situation may be, someone else has overcome much worse. Believe that! Your past or present doesn't fully excuse you; it merely gives you an excuse.

On the flipside, there are those who don't want a permanent mate. If you recognize yourself as such but have been taught otherwise and continually have issues in your relationships because you're constantly at odds with your nature—regroup. Unless of course, you're hiding from yourself and the interferences are of your own doing, in which case, a little soul-searching may be in order. However, if you genuinely do not care to have a mate long-term, yet keep smacking your head against the square-peg-round-hole relationship wall, step away. You're not doing yourself or another a favorable service. Others may disagree with your choice, but until others are paying your bills and living your life, you are not beholden to them. This is not meant to sound insensitive, rather it's meant to impart a viable alternative, especially if a life of perceived joy is what you want. Personal bravery is an admirable asset. Fidelity and accountability to oneself is *paramount.*

When dealing with fidelity and relationships we come up against the stereotypical male and female roles in society, which have in fact served a purpose. However, the perpetuation of the unfavorable aspects of these roles seems somewhat divisive. Granted, biologically we are different. We each have our set of precious pendulates that serve a chief function regarding procreation and the human race. We each have additional characteristics that some say are the by-product of DNA and others say are by way of conditioning; the old nature versus nurture argument, heredity vs. environment. Not to add further to that, because pretty much everything has been, but perhaps stepping back and looking at it from another perspective might prove to have some value. For instance, *we're all humans.* We should be allowed to be such. Boys do cry and girls do go to battle. Males can whip up a mean soufflé and females can mow the back forty. As a society we have come a long way toward softening the drawn lines of male/female stereotypes, but there is still plenty of room for improvement. Men should be readily allowed to wholly utilize their body, mind, and spirit in order to prosper in whichever field they find meaningful, fulfilling, and productive. Not just money-focused, extreme competitive or macho-driven professions. Women should be encouraged to boldly go where no man has gone before, and be equitably compensated while they're at it. They shouldn't have to pander to the coy, submissive or sexed-out, self-defeating societal version of the female. By all means, both should highlight their natural physical and mental gifts; be attractive, sexy and ambitious, but *not* to the detriment of nurturing your overall self. Do not allow the stereotypes to define you. If so, he's just another jerk who flashes his money and she's just another bimbo with too much chest—and that's it, the vacuum. If we repeatedly feed into this, we will likely have infidelity as an all-too-familiar foe because those who indulge in misbehavior will generally not be sound, nourished people.

Both genders have not been roundly permitted to explore their merits as just-plain-old-humans-trying-to-be-productive-and-make-their-way-on-the-planet. We have been conditioned to remain in the same mold since time immemorial; some of it good, some not so good. Being attentive to each other's well-being: good, being subservient: not so good. If men and women are to build a just relationship with one another all that finger pointing and false role-playing needs to shift, or else there stands to be a substantial amount of impairment to the psyche, which adversely affects the male/female interaction. No one should feel threatened if the roles switch-up, if it makes for an enriched life. Imagine if the genders were equally balanced; men wouldn't be as cranky and would bitch less about their psycho mates, and women wouldn't be such harpies, complaining that men "don't get it." If we understood each other's place in the world more so, we'd probably have more compassion and empathy for the other and wouldn't resort to indignant aggravation. Yes, it's near impossible when you'd like to throttle someone instead, but that's the most opportune time to employ the sentiment. That's when it's most beneficial and needed, for each party. As an aside: I've heard men say on repeated occasions that women hold all the power, yet women still deem it's a man's world. A thought-provoking paradox. While it's true each gender has their strong suits and should be lauded for such, we could each stand to expand our horizons. We are not each other's enemies and yet we persist in acting this way. If men and women could find a balance in their relationships based on their respective *selves* being stable, it would be profoundly more satisfying all the way around. It's healthiest when individually independent and developed persons come together to join forces, all the while still allowing for their own person to flourish, yet earnestly holding the relationship's common good in mind. Of course, if you can't seem to get there in spite of how hard you try, the relationship may not be the place for you. Choices will have to be made between living in misery with constant friction, exasperation, and antagonism, or releasing yourself in a respectful way, and realizing there's *still* a lot of life to be lived. Forcing yourself to be a participant in an unsatisfying situation will only breed resentment, fidelity's nemesis.

Another thought to consider is the benefit of having friendships with the opposite sex. Men have told me they don't trust other men to maintain platonic friendships with their mate based on their prejudices about their own gender. And, I'm sure based on how they have played the friendship game with ulterior motives in mind. I imagine it could be said for women as well. But this thought isn't allowing for the trustworthiness of the mate. Friendships of this sort are valuable in that one can be exposed to the opposite gender's point of view and input without overreacting and feeling threatened. Of course, friends of the opposite sex should be incorporated into the romantic relationship and not be isolated incidences on any ongoing basis. Then it will appear suspicious and dubious, and then—well, you get the picture.

Sex. Sex is an enhancement to a healthy relationship; it shouldn't be the only thing going or used to control. Its biological, and some would say, biblical, primary function is for reproduction; fortuitously, it's also physically gratifying. Making genuine love is one of life's immense, passion-filled delights. An ebb and flow occurs naturally when all is right in the world, which can be quite satisfactory for both parties. However, when the home front is strained the tempo can be switched up based on mood. Proceed with care and caution. This is a very delicate area where communication is sure to breakdown quickly. For argument's sake, it's probably best to mood up sooner than later. Take time to scrutinize what the causal bottom line may be, then get it out in the open. In the extreme; sex can be manipulated, mistreated and misread by both sexes. Abuse in any form can not be tolerated. It must be dealt with swiftly and adeptly. If your situation is abusive, you must find help at all costs: ***must***. Check your area's resource guide for urgent assistance or call The National Abuse Hotline, 1-800-621-4673. They handle all types of abuse.

On another note, but disconcerting nonetheless, is sexual dysfunction. If this is a recurring theme in your liaison, it bears scrutiny. It could be an actual physical ailment or an emotional one—even for men. Either way, look into it. We're told women's emotions and sex are intertwined, but not enough is stated about men. Emotions do influence men, whether they're aware of it or not. To paraphrase Herb Goldberg, Ph.D., a best-selling author of many well-received books:...sexual dysfunction in men can be an emotional barometer for what is going on in their relationship. In other words, monitor your body's responses. They have something of importance to convey. Take heed and examine closely.

An added sexual divide: when a domestic upset has occurred and has been somewhat worked through, some feel immediate sex is healing and is a continuum of the love bond. Conversely, others would prefer to be given more time to gather themselves and then work into the lovemaking. This can be very confusing and anxiety-inducing if not discussed in an open and honest manner. Many feel they are being punished by not having their need reciprocated, while others become anxious or resentful if pushed. This disconnect can be difficult to voice effectively. Defense mechanisms and hurt feelings instantly come into play. Again, communication and understanding of how each other's process works will help mend this stand-off. By the way, on the subject of foreplay in a committed partnership, it's not just something called into action a few minutes before you want to make your big score (unless you're both wanting a quickie), it starts from the moment you wake up in the morning. It consists of reasonable doses of love, affection, and caring throughout the day, month, year, etc. It is an important through-line, not just something hurriedly thrown together so you can get down to business. Keep this under advisement because it may have an effect on how your mate views intimacy, and that in turn will affect you. If you find yourself at odds, remember sex outside the relationship may be a boost to your ego and libido, but it's a flimsy band-aid for the underlying wounds. Instead of acting out and bringing another individual into the equation, be mindful—use your head, not a new bed, to make vital decisions.

FYI—it would be advantageous for any man or women with a willingness to explore, to peruse Dr. Goldberg's book, The Hazards of Being Male (or any of his other works). I came across it late; thankfully the content is timeless. It helped me to expand my views on the subject of gender stances. Stay objective while you read. It will be worth your effort. I asked Dr. Goldberg what he felt about fidelity. One comment fully resounded with me, "Fidelity stems from desire. Be faithful because of caring." Well said. He also thinks infidelity is a real opportunity for growth. That may sound counterintuitive, but take a closer look. Once the damage has been done and found out, everybody wakes up. It's a rude awakening to be sure, but you unquestionably have each other's direct attention, and clearly there are problems that need tending. It's possible to effectively address these topics and build a strong foundation from there on in, if enough love, consideration, and determination exist. It will be an unsteady road to trust and acceptance, but once on track you have yourself a far more mature and intimate relationship. For examples tune into, *Unfaithful: Stories of Betrayal* on the OWN network. These stories chronicle indiscretions and the road back to redemption; they are enlightening and hopeful for those who need massive doses of both. View with attentive care.

I suppose I wouldn't be exercising objectivity if I didn't acknowledge that there are enduring relationships and marriages that have started out as affairs. I have limited knowledge of only one. Both parties were married to others, met socializing out and about, left their mates, and married. From what I've heard via a dependable third party, the marriage appears to be solid although not trouble-free. I'm actually curious about these types of relationships. There must be some latent ramifications and hurdles ensuing from the unconventional circumstances, or so I believe. I'd like to hear some stories. Anyone?

Society as a whole has tried to direct laws and ethics in a manner that will best provide for its citizens, yet something is notably missing where fidelity is concerned. There was a day when adultery was a sufficient reason for grounds for divorce. That went by the wayside, in part because trying to attach fault to one party or the other proved to be convoluted and time-consuming. He said/she said, and all else that goes along with it. Family law attorneys have said divorces of this nature used to clog up the system. This is one reason why the no-fault divorce came about. Interesting, as it would seem the inordinate amount of divorces now under the gavel are causing the same amount of congestion, if not more.

Here are some items for deliberate contemplation. Education as a stepping stone; *real-life* education could help pave the way toward fostering healthier individuals, and in turn, relationships. We might begin by addressing this in high school. This is prime-time for hormones, curiosity, and experimentation. Let's find more effective ways to boost the individual and lay the groundwork for prevention. This would be useful on many fronts. We may also be able to reduce unwanted pregnancy, drug use, violence, bullying, etc., if we employ a curriculum that promotes one's sense of self while also stressing the importance of personal accountability. The law as a deterrent: how about creating a new edict to reflect a more proactive stand against infidelity when you're legally bound to another? We make it a tad more difficult to shirk personal and familial responsibilities on a whim. How about people start owning up to their part in extracurricular escapades? What about new rules to include a penalty for the "dissolute damage"? Why not impose at least six months *mandatory* counseling and classes before any divorce will be granted (excluding abuse, etc.)? This may save someone else from having to endure the same behavior, including oneself.

Laws are meant to be fair and just as well as offer protection. In which case, it would stand to reason that should be applicable across the board. Why not also penalize the "other" women/man? They were likewise active participants and are also accountable. It's obvious they could stand a refresher course in fidelity and perhaps a monetary fine to drive the point home. As a strong reprimand, the one who actively *chooses* to stray should categorically pay the higher price—literally. A reasonable cost imposed for the initial offense and up in increments thereafter. Accountability and fines are a main factor for your everyday parking tickets, speeding, DUIs, etc. You do wrong, get caught, receive a ticket, pay the fine, or do the time, which in turn hopefully deters one from being a repeat offender because it doesn't cost *less* to do it again. Why not handle infidelity in somewhat the same manner? After all, the backlash from this is much more far-reaching. It would almost be negligent to continue to do anything less.

Bottom line: *Cheating is Defeating!* Needless to say, it's time for weighty changes. Let's aggregate our considerable resources and do one better. It's time we negotiated a more (re)liable and solid agenda to safeguard fidelity. It's time for a resurgence of our best selves.

Be fearless. Be resolute. *Be* the change-up!

Resource Guide

Those listed here gave of their skill and time to further my goal. They each contributed in their own unique way, whether they realize it or not. I trust they will do the same for you. Feel free to contact me (**www.eldamlopez.com**) with any questions you may have regarding their services.

Aaron Ganz - Social Media Management:
ganzmedia.com

Craig Copeland – Implementation Strategist:
craigcopeland.net

Dan Poynter – Author/ Lecturer:
parapublishing.com

David Lopez – Web Designer/Music Services:
crazyeye.com

Elizabeth A. Garcia – Coach for Success:
mycoachliz.com

Federico Lopez – Photographer; back cover:
freddylopez.com

Gabriella West – Book Editor:
gabriellawest.net

Hazel Palache – Small Business Coach:
yourstairwaytowealth.com

Rick Frishman - Author/ Publisher/Speaker:
rickfrishman.com

Soren Sorenson – Life and Relationship Coach:
spiralgarden.com

Steven W. Booth – Book Formatting:
geniusbookservices.com

Zdenka Hudakova – Book Cover Designer:
zdenka-hudakova.com

About the Author

Elda M. Lopez was reared in Norwalk, CA, studied at the University of Copenhagen, Denmark, and graduated with a B. A. in Theatre Arts from Whittier College. The bulk of her working life was spent in the entertainment business. She currently resides in the Brentwood neighborhood of Los Angeles.

In her new role as an author, Elda's sights are set on addressing infidelity in a more proactive manner via awareness, education, and personal accountability. She has intimate knowledge of this topic which allows for an authentic viewpoint and dialogue.

Her mission and the message are the same: Time for a big change-up!

Please visit us and share your stories or comments at:

http://eldamlopez.com
http://twitter.com/eldamlopez
http://facebook.com/elda.m.lopez

Book available online @ Amazon and Barnes & Noble.